Satipaṭṭhāna Sutta Discourses

S.N. GOENKA

Satipaṭṭhāna Sutta Discourses

Talks from a course in
Mahā-satipaṭṭhāna Sutta

condensed by Patrick Given-Wilson

Vipassana Research Publications • Onalaska

Vipassana Research Publications
867 Larmon Road
Onalaska, WA 98570, USA

First edition: 1998
Second edition: 2015

ISBN: 978-1-938754-90-6 (print)
ISBN: 978-1-938754-87-6 (ePub)
ISBN: 978-1-938754-88-3 (Mobi)
ISBN: 978-1-938754-89-0 (PDF)

Library of Congress Catalog Number: 2015934512

Publisher's Cataloging-in-Publication Data:

Goenka, Satyanarayana, 1924-2013
Satipaṭṭhāna sutta discourses : talks from a course in Mahā-satipaṭṭhāna Sutta / S.N. Goenka ; condensed by Patrick Given-Wilson. — 2nd ed.
p. cm.
LCCN: 2015934512
ISBN: 978-1-938754-90-6

1. Tipiṭaka. Suttapiṭaka. Dīghanikāya. Mahāsatipaṭṭhānasutta—Criticism, interpretation, etc. 2. Tipiṭaka. Suttapiṭaka. Dīghanikāya. Mahāsatipaṭṭhānasutta—Meditations. 3 . Buddhism—Doctrines. I. Given-Wilson, Patrick. II. Title.

Printed in the United States of America

Contents

Introduction vii

Note on the Pronunciation of Pāli xiii

DAY ONE 1

The Three Steps 2

Sati—Awareness 5

Pariyatti—Theoretical Knowledge 8

DAY TWO 13

Ānanda 15

Kurū 18

The Opening Words 20

DAY THREE 25

The Four *Satipaṭṭhānas* 25

Ānāpānapabbaṃ—Observation of Respiration 28

Iriyāpathapabbaṃ—Postures of the Body 34

Sampajānapabbaṃ—Constant Understanding of Impermanence 35

DAY FOUR 39

Paṭikūlamanasikārapabbaṃ—Reflections on Repulsiveness 42

Dhātumanasikārapabbaṃ—Reflections on Material Elements 44

Navasivathikapabbaṃ—Nine Cemetery Observations 45

DAY FIVE 51

Vedanānupassanā—Observation of Sensations 52

Cittānupassanā—Observation of Mind 56

Dhammānupassanā—Observation of Mental Contents 59

Nīvaraṇapabbaṃ—The Hindrances 60

DAY SIX 65

Khandhapabbaṃ—The Aggregates 65

Āyatanapabbaṃ—The Sense Doors 68

Bojjhaṅgapabbaṃ—The Factors of Enlightenment 71

Questions and Answers 76

DAY SEVEN 81

Catusaccapabbaṃ—The Four Noble Truths 81

Dukkhasaccam—The Truth of Suffering 83

Samudayasaccaṃ—The Truth of Arising of Suffering 85

Nirodhasaccaṃ—The Truth of Cessation of Suffering 89

Maggasaccaṃ—The Truth of the Path 90

Satipaṭṭhānabhāvanānisaṃso—Results of the Practice 94

Questions and Answers 97

Glossary 107

Pāli Passages Quoted In the Discourses 122

English Translation of Pāli Passages 123

Contact Information for Vipassana Centers 126

Introduction

S.N. GOENKA, or Goenkaji as he is widely and respectfully referred to, passed away on September 29th, 2013. He was renowned in numerous countries of the world as a master teacher of meditation.

He received the technique that he taught in the 1950s from Sayagyi U Ba Khin of Burma, who had in turn received it from Saya Thet Gyi, who had received it from the Venerable Ledi Sayadaw, a monk who had received it from his own teacher, in a lineage of teachers descended directly from the Buddha. The preservation of the technique through such a long period of time is extraordinary and a cause for gratitude in those who practice it. In a world hungry for inner peace, there was a remarkable spread of the technique during Goenkaji's lifetime: today, Vipassana courses are given in over 150 meditation centers as well as many temporary sites in India and around the world, attracting growing numbers (now about 100,000 people annually).

Despite his magnetic personality, Goenkaji gave credit for the success of his teaching to the efficacy of Dhamma itself. He never sought to play the role of a *guru* or to found any sect, cult or religious organization. He never omitted to say that he received the technique from the Buddha through a chain of teachers down to his own teacher, and to express his gratitude to them for the benefits that he had personally gained in his own meditation. He continually emphasized that he did not teach Buddhism or any kind of "ism," that instead he taught a universal technique which could be practiced by people from any religious or philosophical background or belief.

The standard meditation course in this tradition is a ten days' residential course. Participants commit themselves to staying on the course site for the full ten days, observing a rigorous timetable, maintaining silence for the first nine days. At the beginning of the course, they take the Five Precepts of moral conduct, as given by the Buddha to householders; that is, they undertake to refrain from killing, to refrain from stealing, to refrain from telling lies, to refrain from sexual misconduct (which involves the maintenance of complete celibacy for the duration of the course), and to refrain from taking any intoxicants. They start with the practice of *Ānāpāna* meditation, that is, the observation of the natural breath. On the fourth day, when some concentration has developed, they switch to the practice of Vipassana, the systematic observation of the entire mind-matter phenomenon through the medium of bodily sensations. On the last full day, they practice *Mettā-bhāvanā*, that is, loving kindness, or sharing the merits that they have gained with others.

Although his family was from India, Goenkaji was brought up in Burma (today Myanmar), where he learned the technique from his teacher Sayagyi U Ba Khin. After U Ba Khin authorized him as a teacher, he left Myanmar in 1969 in response to his mother's illness, to give a ten-day course for his parents and twelve others in Bombay (Mumbai). The inspiration that he aroused and the extraordinary results of his teaching led to many more such courses, first in sites around India and then later in permanent meditation centers as they were established. From 1979 onwards he also gave courses outside India, notably in Sri Lanka, Thailand, Nepal, France, the U.K., North America, Japan, Australia and New Zealand. All of these areas today have one or more centers.

In the early days of Goenkaji's teaching, some meditators were confused about how to practice Vipassana. The question arose as to what was Vipassana and what was *Satipaṭṭhāna*. In fact Vipassana and *Satipaṭṭhāna* are synonymous. They are the same.

In order to dispel this misunderstanding and to enable meditators to work directly with the Buddha's words, Goenkaji gave the first *Satipaṭṭhāna Sutta* course at Dhammagiri, the main center near Mumbai, from December 16 to 22, 1981.

The discipline and timetable of a ten-day course remained unchanged, but the participants could study the text of the *Sutta* in the break periods if they wished. Goenkaji's evening discourses explained and expanded on the *Sutta*. In this way *pariyatti* (the theoretical study of Dhamma) and *paṭipatti* (the actual practice of Dhamma) were beneficially combined.

Each of the chapters of this book is a condensed version of the daily evening discourse given by Goenkaji during a *Satipaṭṭhāna Sutta* course held at Dhamma Bhūmi, Blackheath, Australia, in November 1990. The book is intended as a companion volume to the *Mahā-satipaṭṭhāna Sutta*, The Great Discourse on the Establishing of Awareness, with its introduction and notes, published by the Vipassana Research Institute in 1998. That publication contains the full text of the *Sutta* and is used as a handbook by meditation students who are attending the course. The condensed discourses in this book contain only short excerpts from the *Sutta* and it is not intended to be used during the course, when students are able to hear the original discourses directly. It may, however, serve as an aid to meditators after the course as a review of the content, an aid to further study of the texts for scholars, and a tool to assist with translation and better understanding for the benefit of those whose mother tongue is not English.

"Liberation can only be gained by practice, never by mere discussion." These words of Goenkaji give a fitting background to the origin and reason for these discourses and for the *Satipaṭṭhāna Sutta* course itself.

Goenkaji always emphasized the importance of the actual practice of meditation; theory and study were understood as a support to the practice. In the *Satipaṭṭhāna* discourses, he warned of how unfortunate it would be if a center became devoted only to the study of theory. On *Satipaṭṭhāna* courses, as with the ten-day courses, the full meditation timetable is followed, the discourses being restricted just to one period in the evening. This means that the participants can use the theory as a foundation from which to investigate and experience realities inside themselves directly, rather than being caught up in mere abstract debates.

It is not that intellectual study is discouraged but, as Goenkaji emphasized, theory and practice should go together. Similarly, on a ten-day course, the teachings in the discourses proceed from *sīla* (morality) to *samādhi* (mastery of the mind) to *paññā* (wisdom through insight) as the meditators are introduced to each at a practical level.

A prerequisite for the *Satipaṭṭhāna* course in this tradition is the completion of three ten-day courses, regular daily practice and at least a minimum maintenance of *sīla* by keeping the Five Precepts. It is noteworthy that the *Sutta* itself contains no mention of *sīla*. Goenkaji explains the background in the Day Two discourse: the *Sutta* was given to the people of Kuru, who already had a strong background of *sīla*, going back generations. To talk of *sīla* to them was unnecessary; its importance was already understood and assumed. It is also important today that meditators taking this course and working with this *Sutta* have at least a basic understanding and practice of *sīla*. Without this foundation of morality, it is impossible for them to go to sufficient depth in their practice to work effectively with the teaching in the *Sutta*. Many of the original audience of the *Sutta* were already highly developed in their own meditation, needing very little guidance to be able to develop further. While such attainments are not necessarily expected today, a requirement of the course is that the *Satipaṭṭhāna* students at least have some solid experience in this meditation, as well as familiarity with the discourses from a ten-day course.

It was also no coincidence that Goenkaji's teaching of the first course in the *Satipaṭṭhāna Sutta* at Dhammagiri was immediately followed by his teaching of a one-month Vipassana course. The further understanding gained from attending a *Satipaṭṭhāna* course forms an essential base for practice during a long course, and is in fact a requirement for taking long courses in this tradition. This understanding forms a very important and helpful guide for the meditator during the extended solitude spent in practice on a long course. Additionally, the long course discourses refer frequently to the teachings of this important *Sutta*, which are also echoed in many other *suttas*.

All the thousands of discourses given by the Buddha have a particular meaning and inspiration. Each was uniquely tailored by the Buddha to its specific audience, to suit the listeners' situation and level of understanding at that time. The understanding of even one or a few discourses was often sufficient for a meditator to reach the final goal. Nevertheless, this particular discourse has been singled out for intensive study because, given the developed nature of its original audience, it dispenses with many preliminaries and deals in detail with the technique of meditation itself. As such, it is particularly helpful to matured students who wish to study and understand the technique more deeply at the theoretical level in order to strengthen their practice.

The first *Satipaṭṭhāna Sutta* course lasted only eight days because this was the time Goenkaji needed to expound and explain the *Sutta* in the evening discourses. This remains the standard length of the course today. The emphasis therefore is on understanding the *Sutta* and grasping its implications by at least some practice. The practice is then further developed in the long courses after it has been solidly anchored in a deeper knowledge of the theory.

It is a source of great inspiration to students on the course to hear the direct words of the Buddha, in a context where they can work with them directly. Many meditators, having practiced even a little, are thrilled when they first hear the Buddha's words. They straightaway start to understand them in a way that is simply not possible for anyone who has not practiced, because the experiential level is missing from the comprehension of a non-meditator. Many course participants report that they feel as if the Buddha is speaking to them personally, as if his words were meant for them. It is a characteristic of an enlightened person's teachings that they seem to directly address the experience of every meditator.

In the original *Mahā-satipaṭṭhāna Sutta*, and frequently in other *suttas* as well, the Buddha used repetition both for emphasis and clarity.

In his discourses on the *Sutta*, Goenkaji recites each passage in Pāli in its entirety with the same effect. The resonance of the Buddha's original words—especially when recited by Goenkaji, a master teacher of Vipassana—directly invites the listener to deeper meditation. However to produce a written version including all the Pāli that Goenkaji actually recites would risk presenting an unnecessary mass of material, creating difficulties for a reader. This volume therefore separates the discourses and the full text. The discourses contain only excerpts from the *Sutta*, which are then followed by Goenkaji's commentary. For the convenience of the reader, many repeated passages within the excerpts have been omitted and are indicated by ellipsis points (...).

The complete Pāli text and translation appear in the companion volume, the *Mahā-satipaṭṭhāna Sutta*, The Great Discourse on the Establishing of Awareness. In this way, the *Sutta* can be read in its entirety with the background and understanding gained by first reading these condensed discourses. Those who wish to gain the inspiration of hearing the Pāli in full while actually practicing may listen to recordings of Goenkaji's own original discourses or recitation.

No summary of this kind can ever capture in full the flavor and impact of the original discourses. To have been present and to have heard such discourses in person was a great privilege and a source of extraordinary inspiration. The condensed discourses attempt to retain this flavor and atmosphere. While cleaving to Goenkaji's original words where possible, they attempt to distill and crystallize the meaning of each of his points with maximum clarity. If they can serve as an inspiration to all who read them to meditate at deeper levels on the path to liberation, their purpose will have been achieved.

-Patrick Given-Wilson
Dhamma Bhūmi
Blackheath, Australia
February 2015

Note on the Pronunciation of Pāli

Pāli was a spoken language of northern India in the time of Gotama the Buddha. It was written in the Brahmī script in India in the time of Emperor Asoka and has been preserved in the scripts of the various countries where the language has been maintained. In Roman script the following set of diacritical marks are used to indicate the proper pronunciation.

The alphabet consists of forty-one characters: eight vowels and thirty-three consonants.

Vowels: a, ā, i, ī, u, ū, e, o

Consonants:

Velar:	k	kh	g	gh	ṅ
Palatal:	c	ch	j	jh	ñ
Retroflex:	ṭ	ṭh	ḍ	ḍh	ṇ
Dental:	t	th	d	dh	n
Labial:	p	ph	b	bh	m
Miscellaneous:		y, r, l, v, s, h, ḷ, ṃ			

The vowels **a, i, u** are short; **ā, ī, ū** are long:

a is pronounced like 'a' in 'about'; **ā** like 'a' in 'father';
i is pronounced like 'i' in 'mint'; **ī** like 'ee' in 'see';
u is pronounced like 'u' in 'put'; **ū** like 'oo' in 'pool';
e and **o** are pronounced long except before double consonants: *deva, mettā; loka, phoṭṭhabbā.*.

The consonant **c** is pronounced as in the 'ch' in 'church'. All the aspirated consonants are pronounced with an audible expulsion of breath following the normal unaspirated sound. Therefore **th** is not as in 'three' but more like the sound in 'Thailand', and **ph** is not as in 'photo' but rather is pronounced 'p' accompanied by an expulsion of breath.

The retroflex consonants—**ṭ, ṭh, ḍ, ḍh, ṇ**—are pronounced with the tip of the tongue turned back, whereas in the dentals—**t, th, d, dh, n**—it touches the upper front teeth.

The palatal nasal, **ñ**, is the same as the Spanish 'ñ', as in señor. The velar nasal, **ṅ**, is pronounced like 'ng' in 'singer' but occurs only with the other consonants in its group: *ṅk, ṅkh, ṅg, ṅgh.* The pronunciation of the nasal **ṃ** is similar to **ṅ** but occurs most commonly as a terminal nasalization: *'evaṃ me sutaṃ'*. The Pāli **v** is a soft 'v' or 'w' and **ḷ**, produced with the tongue retroflexed, is almost a combined 'rl' sound.

There are a few instances of Sanskrit words in the text. The following are diacritical characters that occur in Sanskrit but not in Pāli:

ṛ is the vocalic 'r', pronounced as 'ri' with a rolled 'r'
ṣ is a retroflex 'sh';
ś is a palatal 'sh'.

Namo tassa bhagavato arahato
sammā-sambuddhassa

DAY ONE

THE FIRST DAY of the *Satipaṭṭhāna* course is over. The technique, and your practice, remain the same. It is however a special course in the sense that you will try to understand the words of the Buddha with reference to the technique. All the teachings, all the discourses of the Buddha are so enlightening, full of wisdom, so precious, just like portions of a big, sweet cake. Every one of them gives the same taste of nectar, ambrosia. The *Mahā-satipaṭṭhāna Sutta* however is chosen because it deals with this technique in detail.

It is better for serious old students to hear the actual words of the Buddha, to understand both practice and theory more clearly, in more detail, and to come out of any confusion. A few enthusiastic students unfortunately started teaching without proper training or grounding in the technique, and mixed other things with it. In India they attended just a few courses. They mostly had great attachment to their own sectarian philosophical beliefs and no technique of their own. With only superficial knowledge of Vipassana, they were unable to teach it properly. Vipassana students who attended their courses got very confused.

Similarly in the West, people have started teaching with a base of this technique, but differently. Just to differentiate they claim to teach *Satipaṭṭhāna,* and say that what Goenka teaches is Vipassana. This caused great confusion. *Satipaṭṭhāna* is Vipassana. Vipassana is *Satipaṭṭhāna.* The direct words of the Buddha will clarify this. They will give inspiration and guidance, and the understanding of Dhamma at a deeper level. Therefore the technique remains the same but the evening discourses will cover this very important *Satipaṭṭhāna Sutta* in detail.

Initially Pāli, the ancient language spoken by the Buddha, will seem very new to you. Slowly you will start understanding the words. Later you will be able to develop a working knowledge of the language. Then it becomes so inspiring. If you are a good Vipassana meditator you will feel as if the words are for you, that the Buddha himself is directing your practice. At this beginning stage, understand just a few words, which will be helpful.

The Three Steps

There are three aspects, or important steps of Dhamma. The first is *pariyatti:* sufficient intellectual knowledge of the teaching. Those who have not even heard or read the words of the Enlightened Person cannot understand Dhamma and its universal nature. They will understand Dhamma only as Buddhist religion. They will take it as a sectarian philosophical belief, or a rite, ritual, or religious ceremony, such as they themselves remain involved in. A *sutavā* is one who has heard and will understand Dhamma as universal law, truth, nature, not limited to any sect or community. Having heard, a *sutavā* can practice and apply it in life, and so is a fortunate person compared to an *assutavā,* who has heard nothing about universal truth, and remains confused.

Hearing or reading words of pure Dhamma is very good to give inspiration and guidance to start practicing. However if you remain satisfied just with that and don't practice, because now you feel you know everything at the intellectual level, then it becomes just a devotional game. Actually you don't know because direct experience is missing. You have just accepted the truth without practicing, which may even become a hindrance to liberation. Therefore every *sutavā* must start practicing.

Paṭipatti, the next step, is practicing Dhamma. In another discourse the Buddha said:

Supaṭipanno Bhagavato sāvaka-saṅgho.

Sāvaka means *sutavā. Sāvaka-saṅgho* means the *saṅgha* which is *sāvaka,* which has heard the teaching of the Buddha and started walking on the path properly—that is, *supaṭipanno,* "well practiced." Walking on the path they will reach the final destination of full liberation. *Paṭipatti* will do this, not *pariyatti* alone. With *pariyatti* you start understanding that as a human being, as a social being, you must live a life of morality in your family and in society. If you disturb the peace and harmony of others, how can you experience peace and harmony? So you abstain from any physical or vocal action which hurts and harms other beings. You abstain from killing, stealing, sexual misconduct, lying, harsh words, backbiting or useless, meaningless words which waste your time and that of others, and from taking any kind of intoxicant. You also understand that by abstaining from unwholesome actions you are actually obliging yourself, not only others. Such unwholesome actions cannot be performed unless you generate great impurity in the mind; like craving, greed, aversion, ego, and fear. When you do that, you harm yourself. For this reason you understand the importance of *sīla,* which means "morality."

However even with your intellectual understanding, maintaining *sīla* becomes difficult without control over the mind. Therefore you must practice *samādhi,* that is mastery of the mind. In certain circumstances, such as the environment of a Vipassana course, it is easy not to break your *sīla,* but walking on the path you have to develop this mastery. You start becoming *supaṭipanno.* Now you are practicing using *Ānāpāna*, awareness of your respiration, which is *paṭipatti.*

As you proceed on the path properly, as an enlightened person intends you to, you have to control the mind in a proper way, or this control will not take you to the third step of *paṭivedhana*. Literally this means "piercing, penetrating." Your *samādhi* concentrates the mind on the reality pertaining to yourself, your own mind-matter phenomenon, because respiration is related to both mind and matter. However, as you proceed you will notice a great stock of accumulated impurities inside. Although you try to control your physical and vocal actions, yet you get overwhelmed by them from time to time. Therefore you have to reach that depth of truth which will take these impurities out.

Paññatti is apparent truth: it seems to be, it appears to be so. To witness ultimate truth you have to remove this curtain of apparent truth, pierce, penetrate, and cut it asunder. This is Vipassana. In another text it was said:

Paññatti ṭhapetvā visesena passatī' ti vipassanā.

Paññatti ṭhapetvā means "having removed the apparent truth." Then Vipassana sees *(passati)* things by their characteristic *(visesena)*. By piercing, penetrating the apparent, solidified, intensified truth, which has to be dissected, disintegrated, dissolved, you move towards the ultimate truth of what is called "I," "mine," the material structure, the mental structure, and the mental contents. Then piercing the entire field of mind and matter you can witness something beyond—the ultimate truth of *nibbāna,* which is eternal, beyond the entire field of mind and matter. This practice of piercing wisdom, *paṭivedhana,* which is Vipassana, leads to the final goal of full liberation.

Therefore understand that the purpose of hearing this *Sutta* during the course is not merely for *pariyatti*. However helpful this theoretical knowledge might be, all three steps of *pariyatti*, *paṭipatti*, and *paṭivedhana* have to be taken. These three cover the entire universe of *paññā*, that is wisdom.

In ten-day courses you have heard about the three stages of *paññā*. *Suta-mayā paññā* is what you have heard. It is someone else's wisdom, not yours. *Cintā-mayā paññā* is your intellectual reasoning, your understanding of someone else's wisdom. Both are good, but only if you take the third step of *bhāvanā-mayā paññā,* to witness the truth yourself. Repeated witnessing develops your wisdom and it is this direct experience that takes you to the final goal.

Different words for this threefold distinction are used in another Indian tradition. First is *sadda sacca,* truth of the word. Fanatics think that the truth of the scriptures must be accepted even without understanding it. When witnessed, experienced, it may be true, but they have merely heard and developed attachment. It is not truth for them. Next is *anumāna sacca,* intellectual understanding by inference. From smoke you infer fire. You have not seen the fire. Both of these can be illusionary, delusionary.

Third is the truth you directly witness yourself: *paccakkha sacca.* The entire teaching of an enlightened person is to inspire you to do this. Belief in the Buddha's words is essential, but unless you yourself witness the truth you can never become enlightened. To listen and understand intellectually is very helpful, but at the same time every teaching has to be witnessed by those who aspire to get liberated. This is what is taught in the *Satipaṭṭhāna Sutta,* and its every word should inspire and guide you.

Sati—Awareness

Sati means awareness, the witnessing of every reality pertaining to mind and matter within the framework of the body. Only with proper understanding and wisdom does it become *satipaṭṭhāna. Ṭhāna* means getting established. *Paṭṭhāna* means getting established in a proper way, which is in different ways, or *pakārena:*

> *Pakārena jānātī'ti paññā.*

Paññā, wisdom, *jānāti,* understands, reality from different angles. Witnessing from only one angle is partial, distorted truth. You have to try to witness the totality, which is done by observing from different angles. Then it is *pakārena,* and it becomes *paññā.*

Thus *sati* becomes *paṭṭhāna* when it is joined with *paññā.* Whenever the Buddha uses the words *sati* or *sato,* he also uses *sampajāno,* as in the *Sutta:*

ātāpī sampajāno satimā

Ātāpī means "ardently." However *sati* is perfect only with wisdom, *sampajāno,* with the understanding of the nature of reality at the experiential level—that is, its basic characteristic of *anicca,* arising and passing. Because its nature is to be impermanent, the characteristic of *dukkha,* misery or suffering, is also inherent. Practicing with *paññā,* you will understand *dukkha* with your own experience. Every pleasant experience, every pleasant situation is *anicca.* Everything within the framework of the body changes into something unpleasant, so it is nothing but *dukkha.* The law of nature is such. Yet the tendency of the mind is to get attached and cling to a pleasant experience, and when it is gone you feel so miserable. This is not a philosophy but a truth to be experienced by *paṭivedhana:* dividing, dissecting, disintegrating, dissolving you reach the stage of *bhaṅga,* total dissolution. You witness the solidified, material structure, the body, as actually nothing but subatomic particles, *kalāpas,* arising and passing. Similarly the mind and mental contents manifest as very solidified, intensified emotions—anger, fear, or passion—which overpower you. Vipassana, *paṭivedhana,* helps you. With piercing, penetrating *paññā* you divide, dissect, disintegrate to the stage where this intense emotion is nothing but wavelets. The whole material and mental structures and the mental contents are nothing but wavelets, wavelets, *anicca, anicca.*

Then the reality about this "I" or "mine" or "myself" becomes clear. They are just conventional words. There is no "I" to possess this mind-matter structure, these material and mental phenomena. Mere mind and matter constantly interact, constantly influence each other, and become a cause for the arising of each other, resulting in currents, crosscurrents, and undercurrents going on in what you call "I." *Anattā* becomes clear at the experiential level.

Anicca, dukkha, anattā—that is, impermanence, misery, and egolessness—should not just be taken as a sectarian philosophy. They don't apply just to Buddhists. Everyone, man or woman, of any color or religion, is merely a constant interaction of mind and matter. Out of ignorance, enormous attachment develops to this false ego, this "I," which brings nothing but misery.

The law of nature becomes so clear with *paṭivedhana*, with piercing, penetrating *paññā*. Without this, mere awareness will not help because you will always remain with the apparent truth, and you won't understand the real, ultimate truth. A circus girl on a tightrope is very aware of every step she takes. Her life and parts of her body are in danger. Still she is far from liberation, because she is only with apparent truth, not with *paññā* inside. The *sati* is not perfect, because it has to be established with the wisdom of *anicca, dukkha, anattā* at the experiential level. *Satipaṭṭhāna* is *sati* with *paññā*. Then it plays a very important part in the practice of Dhamma, of witnessing the truth. The *Satipaṭṭhāna* discourse is for this purpose.

In the ordinary ten-day discourses, you hear of five friends: *saddhā*, faith; *viriya*, effort; *sati*, awareness; *samādhi*, concentration; and *paññā*, wisdom. They were called *indriyas* by the Buddha. *Indra* means "ruler," "king." It is the name of the king of the celestial world. The sense doors are one type of *indriya:* the eyes, ears, nose, tongue and body. They are called this because they keep mastering and overpowering us. The five friends, or faculties which we master, are another type, and *sati* is one of these. These *indriyas* were also called "forces" or "strengths" (*balas*). For every meditator these five are very important strengths, and *sati* is among them. It is so important. *Sati* is also a very important factor of enlightenment. With every one of the seven factors of enlightenment you start with awareness, and you are aware of it till you reach the final goal. However *sati* is important and fruitful only if used properly, as explained by the Buddha in the teachings of this *Satipaṭṭhāna Sutta.*

Pariyatti—Theoretical Knowledge

Tomorrow we will start reading this *sutta.* The background given today is to help you understand that practice is most important. There is a great danger that just reading or hearing *suttas* or discourses may become a life aim. Great care should be taken that the purpose of a Vipassana center remains *paṭipatti* and *paṭivedhana,* the wisdom that is developed and multiplied by experience: little by little, step by step, as you divide, dissect, disintegrate, dissolve and piercingly, penetratingly move from the apparent truth towards the ultimate truth.

One reason, out of many, why Vipassana got lost in India after the time of the Buddha was because theory and *suttas* alone were given importance. People felt satisfied just reciting a discourse, or reciting, memorizing the entire *Tipiṭaka*—the teachings of the Buddha—as if the purpose of their life was fulfilled. Then came discussions, debates, arguments about the meaning of words. Confusion prevailed, and without practice there was no understanding. The words of an enlightened person are words of experience, to guide people to witness the truth. Playing games with them creates a great hindrance. Therefore we use the Buddha's words to understand how he wanted us to practice. They give inspiration and guidance, but the actual practice remains predominant.

Of course we are not denouncing *pariyatti*. How can one who is practicing what the Buddha taught be against the words of the Buddha? However the practice, not the words, should remain the main aim of our life. We are very thankful to the Saṅgha who maintained the purity of the words of the Buddha and those among them who maintained the practice of Vipassana; otherwise it would have been lost long ago. Because of this tradition of ours we received the practice in its pristine purity and we are deeply grateful. Similarly we have great gratitude to those who, whether or not they practiced, at least maintained the words of the Buddha from teacher to pupil for twenty-five centuries.

Now so many queries arise about the Buddha's teaching. Is this the Buddha's teaching or not? Proof is possible only because of those in the Saṅgha of this school who felt responsible for keeping the Buddha's words intact. So they are called *Dhammabhaṇḍāgārikas*, treasurers of the Dhamma—that is, of the words of the Buddha. As a result we can compare the words with the results from the practice of the technique.

Therefore let both *pariyatti* and *paṭipatti* be joined together. *Pariyatti* gives us confidence that our practice is as the Buddha wanted, in the proper way.

Now this *Satipaṭṭhāna Sutta* will be studied. If someone wants to study the entire *Tipiṭaka* it is wonderful. Every word is nectar, gives personal guidance, and is so clear and inspiring. However this is not necessary. Proper understanding of a few *suttas* is good enough. The Buddha said that even one *gāthā* or verse of two lines, if understood properly, is good enough for the final goal. A literal meaning of *pariyatti*, or *pariyapti* in Sanskrit and Hindi, is "sufficient." For some a larger number of discourses is sufficient. The words of the Buddha that you get in the evening discourses on a course are *pariyatti*. You understand how to practice properly, and why in this way, and you develop confidence in the steps you are taking. A few *suttas*, discourses, can be discussed in the evening discourses at centers, for understanding, but that should not be the main aim. Otherwise they will just become *pariyatti* centers: for teaching the *Tipiṭaka*, for discussion, recitation and debate, and also for emotional, devotional and intellectual games.

This is therefore a warning to those who manage such centers around the world, now and for centuries in the future: it is essential that the teaching and practice of Vipassana always remain the main activity, because the final goal will be reached only when you take steps on the path.

Therefore from tomorrow evening we will recite the *sutta,* to understand *paṭipatti* and *paṭivedhana,* the practical aspect, properly. We are on the right path, a path without diversion or deviation, a straight path to the final goal, without wasting time here and there on side issues.

The practice remains the same. Now you are practicing *Ānāpāna,* observing the truth of the breath. This is *sati.* Breath is the nature of a living being, not merely because a book or your teacher or the Buddha says so. You are witnessing it, coming in, going out, as it is. It is not a breathing exercise. You don't regulate it but just observe. Naturally your mind starts getting concentrated. The breath becomes finer, shorter. Then it just makes a U-turn as it comes in or goes out, and at times it seems to stop. Again a big breath comes, out of hunger for oxygen and you are just aware. Again it becomes short, makes a U-turn, stops. You do nothing. Whether it is a long breath, or a short breath, you are just aware. Of course at times when you can't feel the subtle breath, you may have a few intentional, conscious breaths, just to feel the natural breath again.

This course is only eight days long, so time is short. Use it most seriously. You have a wonderful advantage here in that new students who often don't understand the value of discipline and silence, and who in their confusion disturb others, are not allowed on the course. As mature old students of at least a few courses you understand the work, and you understand that continuity of practice is the secret of success. If you keep stopping your work out of laziness, wandering, roaming about or lying down and sleeping, you can't reach the goal. Of course your mind will wander away, but you bring it back. Your effort must be continuous. Even the so-called recess periods, including the nighttime, are for serious work, for meditation, for awareness. *Sati* must get established—*satipaṭṭhāna.* Now with *Ānāpāna,* you are aware of respiration. Sitting, standing, walking, lying down; bathing, washing, eating, drinking—day and night, except only the period of deep sleep, you are aware of natural breath. The *sati* gets *paṭṭhāna.* Awareness gets well established. Then in Vipassana the awareness, day and night, is of arising and passing, *anicca.*

All the rules are so important. A course like this without new students and with minimum disturbance, where everybody is so serious, is very rare. Make best use of this opportunity, this facility, to get your awareness established with wisdom, to come nearer and nearer to the final goal. Make best use of this wonderful technique. Make best use of Dhamma for your own good, benefit, and liberation from the bondages, shackles and chains of craving, aversion, and ignorance. May you all enjoy real peace, harmony and happiness.

May all beings be happy.

DAY TWO

THE SECOND DAY of the *Satipaṭṭhāna* course is over. This evening we will start to go through the discourse to understand it in relation to the actual practice.

The name of the discourse is *Mahā-satipaṭṭhāna Sutta. Sutta* means discourse. *Mahā* means great, and indeed there is another shorter discourse on *Satipaṭṭhāna.* This present discourse, however, covers more subjects in detail and is therefore called *mahā.*

Sati means awareness. It is a very important faculty of Dhamma, as was discussed yesterday. It is one of the *indriyas,* the faculties to be developed. It is one of the *balas*, the forces, the strengths that must be developed to master Dhamma. It is one of the *bojjhaṅgas,* factors of enlightenment. *Sammā-sati* is part of the Noble Eightfold Path. Its literal meaning, as commonly used nowadays in India as *smṛti,* is "memory" or "remembrance". Vipassana involves no past memory, but you must always remember the object of meditation, which is the reality pertaining to mind and matter within the framework of the body. A better sense or understanding of *sati* is awareness, which is what it is; and awareness has to be of the reality of this moment as it is, of the present, not the past or future.

Paṭṭhāna means getting established. *Pa* means extensively, which includes the element of *paññā,* wisdom. The awareness is not merely of the truth of mind and matter, but also of the nature of this truth: how it arises and passes; how it is a source of misery; how it is not "I," how it is substanceless. Direct experience is required. This is not mere intellectual understanding of an apparent truth. Awareness is established with wisdom, which is the understanding of the true nature of reality. Hence the name *Mahā-Satipaṭṭhāna Sutta.*

The discourse starts:

> *Evaṃ me sutaṃ.*
>
> This was heard by me.

The words are not those of the Buddha. There is a history behind them, which Vipassana meditators should know.

When the Buddha passed away at the ripened age of eighty, his students then present who were *arahants*, fully liberated, understood that everyone, a Buddha or an ordinary person, has to pass away. This is a law of nature. Others of his students who were not developed in Dhamma to this extent felt very sad, and some even cried. However one person, a monk, old in age but not wisdom, dissented. He felt very happy that the old man had passed away: now they were free of his clutches and could do what they liked. The Buddha's own teaching after all was: *Attā hi attano nātho—You are your own master. This incident reveals that elements had already entered the Saṅgha who were not interested in Dhamma. They had come for status, a comfortable life, and more alms and respect than they would receive otherwise.*

I feel very grateful to this monk. Why? When Mahākassapa, a wise, elderly monk, an arahant, fully liberated, and one of the chief disciples of the Buddha, heard this, he decided to preserve the actual teachings of the Buddha against future distortion by such elements. For forty-five years, day and night, the Buddha had taught Dhamma, hardly resting two or three hours at night, and even that not in ordinary sleep but with awareness and equanimity, with wisdom. He had given 82,000 discourses, and his leading *arahant* disciples had given another 2,000. This makes 84,000 in all. Mahākassapa thought that others, like this old monk, would in future misquote the teachings, substituting their own words and removing essential disciplines—all of which did happen. Therefore he decided to call a conference of 500 elderly monks, *arahants* who were eyewitnesses to the Buddha's teaching, to recite, compile and authenticate the actual words. Just a few could have done this, but to impress people and ensure acceptance he took 500 immediately after the Buddha's death. Together they were to recite every word of the Buddha and give it the seal of authenticity.

Ānanda

Ānanda was recommended to him as the 500th member of this gathering. Ānanda was born on the same day as Gotama the Buddha, was his cousin and had spent his childhood and youth with him. When the Buddha became enlightened, Ānanda was one of many family members who renounced the householder's life and joined him. As the number of followers, and so the work, grew, the Buddha needed an assistant. Some came, but with various motives. The usual one was the hope for a private viewing of miracles, although in public the Buddha discouraged miracles. Another was to hear the answers to certain philosophical questions which he would never answer in public. Such people could not stay long, and they left.

As the Buddha grew in age to fifty-five, the need for a stable personal assistant was accepted. Many senior monks were very eager to serve him so closely, but he was known to prefer Ānanda. Yet Ānanda remained silent. He actually asked the Buddha to agree to some terms. There were seven or eight, very healthy terms, and the Buddha accepted all of them. One was that if ever the Buddha gave a discourse at which Ānanda was not present, the Buddha must, on returning, repeat the discourse to him. Thus he heard every discourse for the last twenty-five years of the Buddha's life. He had also heard them before that time. Ānanda had a wonderful faculty of memory due to his practice and past good qualities. If he heard something once, he could repeat it any time, word for word, like a computer or tape recorder today.

Ānanda had served the Buddha for twenty-five years. He had been so close to him, was his great personal devotee, yet he was not an *arahant,* not fully liberated. He was only a *sotāpanna,* having reached the first stage of liberation after the initial experience of *Nibbāna.* Beyond that is the stage of *sakadāgāmī,* then *anāgāmī,* then *arahant.* You should understand from this that a Buddha cannot liberate anyone. Ānanda also knew Dhamma so well: thousands taught by him were *arahants,* yet he was continually serving the Buddha, without the time to progress himself.

So Mahākassapa approached him, saying that now that the Buddha had passed away Ānanda had the time, and as a teacher he himself knew the technique so well. He asked him to work to become an *arahant* and join the gathering since he would be a great asset there. Ānanda gladly agreed; he would practise for a few days, become an *arahant,* and join them.

He started working very vigorously, aiming to become an *arahant.* As a teacher he advised others not to develop ego, as it was a dangerous obstacle. Often the teacher when he practises forgets his own teaching, and this is what happened. His aim was—"I *must* become an *arahant.*" He made no progress. Mahākassapa came and told him that the conference would start the following day, if necessary without him. If he was not an *arahant* they would take someone else. Again he tried the whole night—"I *must* become an *arahant.*" The night passed away and the sun rose. Exhausted from his work, he decided to rest. He didn't cry, he had that good quality. Now he was not aiming to be an *arahant.* He just accepted the fact that he was not an *arahant,* he was only a *sotāpanna.* Like a good meditator, remaining aware of sensations arising and passing, he took rest. His mind was now no longer in the future, but in the reality of the present moment. Before his head reached the pillow, he became an *arahant.*

It is a middle path. With too much laxity you achieve nothing. With overexertion the mind is unbalanced. Ānanda joined the conference.

Now Ānanda was asked exactly what the Buddha had said, and all the teachings were compiled. Three divisions were made, called *Tipiṭaka. Ti* means three, *piṭaka* commonly means basket, though it also refers to scriptures. The first is *Sutta-piṭaka,* the public discourses.

The second is *Vinaya-piṭaka,* the discourses to monks and nuns about discipline and *sīla.* For householders, five precepts, *sīlas,* are good enough, but for the monks and nuns there were over 200 *sīlas,* which is why the old monk dissented.

The third is *Abhidhamma-piṭaka,* higher Dhamma, deeper truths about the laws of nature not easily understood by an ordinary person. It is an analytical study of the entire field of mind and matter with full detail of the reality pertaining to matter *(rūpa)*, mind *(citta)*, and the mental factors, the mental concomitants, the mental contents *(cetasika)*. It fully explains how they interact and influence each other, how matter and mind stimulate the arising of both themselves and each other, and the interconnections, currents, and crosscurrents deep inside. This all becomes clear not just by reading *Abhidhamma,* but only by a deep practice of Vipassana. Ānanda was asked to recite the *Suttas* and *Abhidhamma,* and another *arahant,* perfect in the discipline, Upāli, was asked to recite the *Vinaya.*

This discourse comes in the *Sutta-piṭaka.*

Ānanda starts *Evaṃ me sutaṃ,* "This was heard by me," because he had heard it directly from the Buddha. He also gives an explanation of the situation in which the *Sutta* was given. "At one time the Enlightened One was living *(viharati)* among the Kurūs at Kammāssadhammaṃ, a market town of the Kurū people." Viharati is only used in India for very enlightened persons or those practising Dhamma. Kurū was then one of sixteen states in northern India at that time, now called Haryana, somewhere near Delhi and Punjab. The Buddha called the *bhikkhus,* that is the meditators present, and spoke.

Kurū

The Buddha gave this discourse in Kurū for a reason. Not only the Buddha but others also had high regard for the people of Kurū. In another Indian tradition, the *Bhagavad-Gītā* starts with the words: *Dharmakṣhetre, Kurukṣhetre,* meaning in "the field of Dhamma, the field of Kurū." In another discourse the Buddha explains how the Kurūs lived a life of morality, observing *sīla,* from the king to the lowest subject. This was quite unusual, and what is now called *sīla-dhamma* had then been called *Kurū-dhamma.* Morality was their nature.

At that time, in a past life of the Buddha, the then-*bodhisatta* was the ruler of Kurū. Kaliṅga, another state now called Orissa, was suffering from drought and famine year after year. It was then believed that such famines happened when people did not lead moral lives, because the ruler himself did not live a moral life. The elders of Kaliṅga advised the king to take five precepts, let all his people do the same, and observe them. It was also important that the precepts were taken from someone perfect in them. They recommended the ruler of Kurū, a perfect person, all of whose subjects lived a moral life.

Two brahmin ambassadors were sent. They told the ruler the whole story and asked him to write the precepts down on a slate: on his behalf they would read it out, and people would start practising and so come out of their misery. The ruler of Kurū refused. Although he had been living a perfect life of *sīla,* he felt he had committed one slight mistake. He sent them to his elderly mother. She also said she had made one slight mistake. So they were sent to the chief queen; and similarly, successively to the king's younger brother, to the prime minister, the revenue minister, the chief businessman, down even to the charioteer and the watchman at the gate. All said they had made a slight mistake.

Yet these mistakes were so trivial. For example, the king had been demonstrating his skill in archery. An arrow fell in a pond, and did not float. Perhaps it pierced a fish. Whether it actually did is doubtful. The Kurū people were that careful.

A base of *sīla* is essential. However, in the gap between one Buddha and another, other parts of Dhamma become lost, and this is what had happened. The Dhamma that a Buddha gives is complete and pure—*kevalaparipuṇṇaṃ, kevalaparisuddhaṃ*—with nothing to be added or taken out. As time passes important parts get lost. *Paññā,* the most difficult part, disappears first: only intellectual *paññā* remains. Then pure *samādhi* goes: imaginations remain, but the awareness of reality goes. *Sīla* remains, but when the other steps are lost, it is overemphasised and stretched to such extremes that the mind becomes unbalanced. The same thing happens in India today: people become too unbalanced to practise proper *samādhi* and *paññā.*

The Buddha kept condemning *sīla-vata-parāmāsa. Vata* means a vow. *Parāmāsa* means attachment. Without proper *samādhi* or *paññā,* people take a vow, *vata,* and stretch just one *sīla,* thinking that it will liberate them. There is nothing wrong in *sīla* or *vata,* both are important. A vow not to take meals after midday helps your meditation, or to fast for a day keeps you healthy. But when it becomes stretched people fast for up to a month, just to prove their Dhamma, and the essence, the purpose gets lost.

This was the situation in Kurū at that time. Their *sīla* was good, but had been stretched. Although that was wrong, still observing *sīla* is definitely much better than not observing it. What they lacked in Dhamma, could be gained by the technique. The *Sutta* therefore does not talk of *sīla,* because this strong background was already there. With such a good base, the people of Kurū would understand the details of this technique much better. Therefore the Buddha gave this *Sutta* in Kurū.

Then he addressed the *bhikkhus.* In the ordinary language of India a *bhikkhu* means a monk, a recluse, but in all of the Buddha's teachings a *bhikkhu* means anyone who is practising the teaching of Dhamma. Therefore it means a meditator, whether a householder—man or woman—or a monk or nun.

The Opening Words

Ekāyano ayaṃ, bhikkhave, maggo

This is the one and only path.

Sattānaṃ visuddhiyā: to purify individuals. This at the mental level. Washing the body externally will not purify the mind. The results of this purification follow:

Soka-paridevānaṃ samatikkamāya: transcending very deep sorrow, *soka,* and its manifestation in crying and lamentation, *parideva.* As you practise, it comes to the surface and observing, you pass beyond it, *samatikkamāya.*

Dukkha-domanassānaṃ atthaṅgamāya. At a subtler level there is still unpleasant feeling in the mind, *domanassa,* and unpleasant sensation on the body, *dukkha.* These also are eradicated, *atthaṅgamāya.*

Ñāyassa adhigamāya. Ñāya means truth. If you work with contemplation or imagination such results will not come. Only the surface of the mind is purified. The deepest misery can only be taken out when you observe the reality of mind and matter and their interconnection, from gross apparent truth to the subtlest ultimate truth. The truth experienced by the Buddha can only liberate the Buddha. A Buddha can only show the path, you have to walk on it. *Ñāyassa adhigamāya* is the high road of liberation.

Nibbānassa sacchikiriyāya. Nibbāna has to be experienced, realised, *sacchikiriyāya*, by the observation of truth. You have to reach the subtlest reality of mind and matter and then transcend it to witness something beyond. The entire field of mind and matter is that of *anicca,* arising and passing. At a gross level it arises, seems to stay for some time, and then passes away. At a subtler level, it passes with great rapidity. At the subtlest level there is merely oscillation. The ultimate truth beyond is where nothing arises or passes. It is beyond mind and matter, beyond the entire sensorium, the sensory field. The experience of *nibbāna* can be for a few moments, a few minutes, a few hours; it depends, but you come back a changed person. You can't explain it. Of course people can give long intellectual explanations, but the sense organs stop functioning in *nibbāna.* They cannot be used to explain it. Thus the last of the six qualities of Dhamma is *paccattaṃ veditabbo:* it must be experienced directly and personally by each individual within him- or herself.

Ekāyano maggo, "the one and only path," seems to be narrow-minded. Those who have not walked on the path, or have not walked on it very much, may feel uncomfortable. For those who have walked on it, it is clearly the one and only path. It is after all the universal law of nature. It is to be experienced and understood by everyone, from any religion or country. Fire will burn anyone's hand. If you don't like being burnt, you keep your hand away, whether you are a Buddhist or a Christian, an Australian or an American. The law of gravity exists with or without Newton. The law of relativity exists with or without Einstein. Similarly the law of nature remains whether or not there is a Buddha. It is cause and effect. Two parts of hydrogen and one part of oxygen make water. If either is missing on a planet, there will be no water. This is a law of nature. This is Dhamma. As you proceed—and work much deeper—you will understand this. If you don't want misery, you have to remove the cause. Then the resulting misery is automatically removed.

If you think that some supernatural power will liberate you in spite of all your impurities, it is just wishful thinking. It won't happen. You have to work according to the law of nature. Your present deep habit pattern of reacting out of ignorance, as a result of which you keep experiencing misery, has to be changed.

In this sense it is *ekāyano maggo,* and the Buddha now describes it further.

...yadidaṃ cattāro satipaṭṭhānā: that is to say, the four *satipaṭṭhānas.* At this stage note how there are four *satipaṭṭhānas,* or four ways of establishing awareness with wisdom. The first is:

> *Kāye kāyānupassī viharati ātāpī sampajāno satimā, vineyya loke abhijjhādomanassaṃ.*

Kāye kāyānupassī viharati: to live witnessing the reality of the body in the body. The practice is done *ātāpī,* very ardently, diligently, *sampajāno,* with the wisdom of arising and passing, and *satimā,* with awareness. No imagination is involved, rather direct full awareness, with wisdom. The truth pertaining to the body is observed, experienced within the body itself. This is done *vineyya,* keeping away from, *abhijjhādomanassaṃ,* craving and aversion towards the *loke,* the mind-matter phenomena.

> *Vedanāsu vedanānupassī viharati ātāpī sampajāno satimā, vineyya loke abhijjhādomanassaṃ.*

The second is *vedanāsu vedanānupassī viharati:* to live witnessing the truth of bodily sensations. Again there is no imagination. The truth is observed within the bodily sensations, by direct experience in the same way.

Citte cittānupassī viharati ātāpī sampajāno satimā, vineyya loke abhijjhādomanassaṃ.

Similarly the third is *citte cittānupassī viharati:* witnessing the reality of mind within mind.

Dhammesu dhammānupassī viharati ātāpī sampajāno satimā, vineyya loke abhijjhādomanassaṃ.

The fourth is *dhammesu dhammānupassī viharati:* witnessing the reality of the mental contents, the law of nature, of mind and matter, within the law, within the mental contents. This is done in the same way.

These four *satipaṭṭhānas*, observing the truth of body, or sensations, or mind, or contents of the mind, all have to be directly experienced. Intellectual understanding will give you inspiration and guidance as to how to practise, but only experience will give results. This is to be understood as we proceed.

Now you are working with respiration, the reality of this moment, as it is, coming and going, deep or shallow. You try also to maintain awareness of the reality of sensation in this area of the body, below the nostrils above the upper lip, as it manifests from moment to moment. The object is this area of the body. Try to maintain the continuity of awareness day and night, except when you are in deep sleep. Most of the time the mind will wander. You will forget, you can't help it, but as soon as you realise, bring the mind back. Don't generate disappointment or depression. Just accept that the mind has wandered away, and start again. Work more seriously, more diligently now. Time is very short. You have come to a course with a very serious atmosphere, undisturbed by new students. Make use of it for your own good, benefit and liberation. May you all enjoy real peace, harmony, happiness.

May all beings be happy.

DAY THREE

THE THIRD DAY of the *Satipaṭṭhāna* course is over.

We expressed our gratitude to the old monk because of whom Mahākassapa decided to compile all the teachings. As a result, they were maintained in their pristine purity from generation to generation. Sometimes something very wholesome results from an unwholesome situation. This is what happened. Over the centuries six councils of monks have recited and authenticated the *Tipiṭaka*, to remove any mistakes that had crept in. Three councils were held in India, one in Sri Lanka, and two in Burma. The sixth and most recent was in Rangoon in 1955-56, 2,500 years after the Buddha passed away. Just as we are grateful to those who maintained the practice in its pristine purity, we are also grateful to those who have maintained the purity of the Buddha's words. Today we can compare the words with the technique, and derive more inspiration by knowing that we are practicing as the Buddha taught.

We continue with the discourse.

The Four *Satipaṭṭhānas*

As we discussed, there are four *satipaṭṭhānas*:

kāye kāyānupassī viharati ātāpī sampajāno satimā, vineyya loke abhijjhādomanassaṃ;

vedanāsu vedanānupassī viharati ātāpī sampajāno satimā, vineyya loke abhijjhādomanassaṃ;

citte cittānupassī viharati ātāpī sampajāno satimā, vineyya loke abhijjhādomanassaṃ;

dhammesu dhammānupassī viharati ātāpī sampajāno satimā, vineyya loke abhijjhādomanassaṃ.

The purpose of *satipaṭṭhāna* is to explore the area which is identified with "I," to which so much attachment develops. There are two distinct fields: *kāya* (body) and *citta* (mind).

The exploration must be done at the experiential, not the intellectual, level. If you try to understand body just by taking the attention, say, to the head and asserting that "This is my head," it is only an intellectual truth, that of *saññā* (recognition). To experience reality you must feel it. Therefore there must be sensation, and *kāya* (body) and *vedanā* (sensation) go together in this exploration.

Similarly with *citta:* to sit down and merely assert that this is your mind will only be an imagination or at best an intellectual understanding. To experience mind, something must arise in the mind: perhaps some strong craving or aversion, or some thought. It arises and passes away. Whatever it is is called *dhamma,* the literal meaning of which is *dhāretī ti dhamma,* "that which is contained" by *citta.* Just as *kāya* and *vedanā* go together, *citta* and *dhamma* go together. Then, as the Buddha elsewhere announced from his own experience, another reality: *vedanā-samosaraṇā sabbe dhammā.* "Everything that arises in the mind starts flowing with a sensation on the body." *Samosaraṇā* means "gets collected together and flows."

Vedanā therefore becomes so important. To explore the *kāya* you have to feel sensations. Similarly in the exploration of *citta* and *dhamma,* everything that arises in the mind manifests as a sensation.

Continuing, each *satipaṭṭhāna* has certain similar words:

Kāye kāyānupassī viharati: *anupassī* comes from *passana* or *dassana,* "to look." You see things directly yourself. *Vipassanā* means seeing in a special way, the correct way. *Vividhena* means in different ways, from different angles. *Vicayena* means by dividing, dissecting, disintegrating. So you observe whatever reality has arisen. *Anupassanā* means continuously from moment to moment. Thus *kāye kāyānupassī* is to observe the body from moment to moment within, that is, *in* the body. Similarly *vedanāsu* is *in* the sensations, *citte* is *in* the mind and *dhammesu* is *in* the mental contents.

Vipassana uses no imagination. You could imagine a sensation and that it is changing even without experiencing it, but this is not reality as it is, where it is. Your body must be experienced in your own body, sensations in your own sensations, mind in your own mind, mental contents in your own mental contents. Therefore the meditator lives, dwells observing body in the body, *ātāpī sampajāno satimā.*

Ātāpī literally means *tapas,* "burning." A meditator who is working very ardently, very diligently, burns off the mental impurities. *Satimā* means "aware." *Sampajāno* means having the quality of *sampajañña.* The awareness must be with *sampajañña,* the *paññā* that feels the arising and passing away of *vedanā,* because impermanence has to be experienced at the level of *vedanā.* Thus the observation, whether of *kāya, vedanā, citta,* or *dhammā* must be *ātāpī sampajāno satimā.*

Vineyya loke abhijjhā-domanassaṃ... Keeping away from craving and aversion towards this world of mind and matter.

Vineyya means to keep away from, or to abstain from. *Lokas* are the planes of the universe. Here *loke* means the entire field of mind and matter, all five aggregates which constitute "I": the material aggregate *(rūpa)* and the four mental aggregates of cognizing *(viññāṇa)* recognising *(saññā)* feeling *(vedanā)* and reacting *(saṅkhāra).* All four *satipaṭṭhānas* can be practiced only with the base of *vedanā.* This is because unless something is felt *(vedanā),* craving and aversion *(abhijjhā-domanassaṃ)* cannot arise. If the sensation is pleasant, only then does craving arise; if the sensation is unpleasant, only then does aversion arise. If you don't experience sensations, you won't even know that craving or aversion has arisen, and you can't come out of them.

Ānāpānapabbaṃ— **Observation of Respiration**

In exploring the field of matter, the body (*kāya*), the first chapter is on *Ānāpāna,* the respiration coming in and going out.

Idha, bhikkhave, bhikkhu araññagato vā rukkhamūlagato vā suññāgāragato vā

A place of solitude is required—secluded and with no disturbance. The meditator goes to a forest *(arañña-gato vā)* the foot of a tree *(rukkha-mūla-gato vā)* or a place where nobody lives *(suññāgāra-gato vā),* like the individual cells you have here—any of these three.

nisīdati pallaṅkaṃ ābhujitvā, ujuṃ kāyaṃ paṇidhāya

The meditator must sit down *(nisīdati). Pallaṅkaṃ ābhujitvā* means "cross-legged." The lotus or half-lotus posture is not necessary. If this is possible, it is a posture that brings greater alertness, but otherwise any cross-legged posture that is comfortable for longer periods at a stretch is good enough. The upper portion of the body should be straight: *ujuṃ kāyaṃ paṇidhāya.*

parimukhaṃ satiṃ upaṭṭhapetvā

The awareness is established around the mouth, the entrance to the nostrils: *parimukhaṃ.* Certain traditions translate this as "in the front," as if the awareness is imagined to be in front of the person, but this sets up a duality. Actually you have to feel the breath coming and going around the mouth, above the upper lip, which is *parimukhaṃ.*

Then the work starts:

So sato va assasati, sato va passasati.

With awareness he breathes in, with awareness he breathes out.

Dīghaṃ vā assasanto 'Dīghaṃ assasāmīti' pajānāti, dīghaṃ vā passasanto 'Dīghaṃ passasāmīti' pajānāti.

Breathing in a deep breath *(dīgha)*, he understands properly *(pajānāti)*: "I am breathing in a deep breath." Breathing out a deep breath, he understands properly: "I am breathing out a deep breath." The long inbreath, and similarly the long outbreath, is known and understood as such: because it is felt, experienced.

Rassaṃ vā assasanto 'Rassaṃ assasāmīti' pajānāti, rassaṃ vā passasanto 'Rassaṃ passasāmīti' pajānāti.

Now the breath becomes shallow, short *(rassa)*, and is understood in the same way. You will see how each sentence signifies another station on the path, a new experience. As the mind calms down the agitation decreases, and the breath becomes short. It is not controlled as in a breathing exercise, but just observed.

'Sabbakāyapaṭisaṃvedī assasissāmī' ti sikkhati; 'sabbakāyapaṭisaṃvedī passasissāmī' ti sikkhati.

Now he trains himself: "Feeling the whole body *(sabbakāyapaṭisaṃvedī)*, I shall breathe in, feeling the whole body, I shall breathe out." Instead of *pajānāti*, to understand properly, the word *sikkhati*, "learns, trains" is now used. As meditators, after a day or two's work with the breath, you have experienced sensation in this area. Then working with both you reach the stage of feeling sensation throughout the body—*sabba-kāya*. Initially it is very gross, solidified, intensified, but as you keep practicing patiently, persistently, remaining equanimous with every experience, the whole body dissolves into subtle vibrations, and you reach the stage of *bhaṅga*, total dissolution. Having started with natural breath, you learn to reach the important station of feeling sensations in the whole body in one breath: from top to bottom as you breathe out, from bottom to top as you breathe in.

Without practice there will be confusion. Other traditions interpret these words as "the body of the breath," as if the beginning, middle, end, and so the whole breath is felt. Of course, as oxygen enters the bloodstream with the breath, it moves throughout the body from the top of the head to the toes, and sensation flows with the blood. It could be taken in this sense, but we are practicing *kāyānupassanā.* The whole body must be felt, and this is what a meditator experiences.

When *bhaṅga* comes, following all the unpleasant sensations, the tendency of the mind is to react with craving and clinging. This is a dangerous *(ādīnava)*, fearful *(bhaya)* situation. It is much easier to stop having aversion to unpleasant sensation than to stop having craving towards pleasant sensation. Yet this craving is the mother of aversion, and Vipassana is to work *vineyya loke abhijjhā-domanassaṃ*—without craving or aversion. You have to keep understanding that the pleasant sensation also is *anicca,* nothing but tiny wavelets, bubbles, arising and passing. With this *paññā* the impurities get eradicated and the station of calmness, tranquillity is reached.

> *'Passambhayaṃ kāyasaṅkhāraṃ assasissāmī' ti sikkhati,*
> *'passambhayaṃ kāyasaṅkhāraṃ passasissāmī' ti sikkhati.*

Now with the body activities *(kāyasaṅkhāra)* calmed *(passambhayaṃ)* he trains himself to breathe in and out. Again the word *sikkhati* is used, because this station is reached by learning, by practice. The one hour *adhiṭṭhāna* sitting in which the posture is not changed, which was initially a struggle, becomes natural. There is no movement of the body because there is no unpleasant sensation anywhere. Breath becomes the only movement. This also is a *kāya-saṅkhāra,* a movement or activity of the body. As the mind is trained to become calm and tranquil, the breath also becomes shorter, calmer, subtler until it just makes a U-turn as it enters, and at times it seems to stop. It is so fine. Here also there is the danger of attachment, of taking this as the final stage.

Now the Buddha gives the example of a carpenter, who, then as now, turns and cuts wood, for instance to make a leg for a piece of furniture. He uses a lathe. A long turn of the lathe makes a thicker cut than a short turn. He, or his apprentice, knows well *(pajānāti)* whether his turn is long or short; similarly the meditator knows well *(pajānāti)* whether the breath is long or short.

In the example the lathe cuts at the point of contact. Similarly the attention is to be kept where the breath touches. You should not follow the breath deep inside or outside into the atmosphere. You are aware of this area and you also feel the whole breath coming in or going out.

> *Iti ajjhattaṃ vā kāye kāyānupassī viharati, bahiddhā vā kāye kāyānupassī viharati, ajjhattabahiddhā vā kāye kāyānupassī viharati.*

In the next important station, with the help of the breath the whole body is felt inside, or within oneself, *ajjhattaṃ.* Then it is also felt outside, *bahiddhā,* on the surface of the body, and lastly simultaneously both inside and outside.

These are the Buddha's words. Certain commentaries or subcommentaries have been written on them, some 1,000 to 1,500 years after the Buddha, and some even more recently. They give many good explanations of the Buddha's words, and also descriptions of a whole spectrum of life and society at that time—political, social, educational, and economic aspects. However they give certain interpretations which this tradition of meditation cannot accept. For instance, here a commentary takes *ajjhattaṃ* as the meditator's body—which is acceptable—but *bahiddhā* as the body of someone else, even though no one else is there. It explains that the meditator can simply think of someone else, and how all beings similarly breathe in and out. We cannot agree with this because this is imagination, and in this tradition *vipassanā* or *anupassanā* is to observe *within* your own body *(kāye)*. Therefore for us *bahiddhā* is the surface of the body, but still within its framework.

Ajjhatta-bahiddhā can also be understood in relation to the five sense doors. When an outside object comes into contact with the eyes, ears, nose, tongue, or body surface, it is felt within the framework of the body, but on the surface of the body. Even the mind is within the framework of the body, although its object may be outside. The *Sutta* still does not intend you to start thinking of or seeing another body.

The next few sentences appear in every chapter. They describe the real practice of Vipassana, and great care should be taken to understand them properly.

> *Samudayadhammānupassī vā kāyasmiṃ viharati, vaya-dhammānupassī vā kāyasmiṃ viharati, samudayavaya-dhammānupassī vā kāyasmiṃ viharati...*

Samudaya-dhammānupassī: the *dhamma,* the reality, or the truth of arising *(samudaya)* is observed within the body. Then the truth of passing away *(vaya)* is observed. The gross sensation arises, seems to stay for some time, then passes away. Arising and passing are seen as separate. Then in the stage of *bhaṅga,* total dissolution, the sensation is one of vibrations that arise and pass with great rapidity. *Samudaya* and *vaya* are experienced together: there is no interval. According to the *Visuddhimagga*, the Path of Purification, the first important station is called *udayabbaya*. A meditator must understand this and the next stage of *bhaṅga* well.

> *...'atthi kāyo' ti vā panassa sati paccupaṭṭhitā hoti.*

Now his awareness is established: "This is body" *('atthi kāyo' ti)*. This is the stage in which the body is experienced as "not I," "not mine," but just body, just a mass of vibrations, bubbles, wavelets. It is merely a collection of *kalāpas,* subatomic particles, arising and passing. There is nothing good or bad, beautiful or ugly, white or brown about it. Initially the acceptance of *anattā,* "not I," is intellectual or devotional, based on the words of someone else. The actual experience starts with *anicca,* because every pleasant sensation turns into an unpleasant one. The danger of attachment is realized. It is *dukkha* because of its inherent nature of change. Then *anattā* is understood: the body is felt as just subatomic particles arising and passing, and automatically the attachment to body goes away. It is a high stage when the awareness, *sati,* gets established, *paccupaṭṭhitā hoti,* in this truth from moment to moment.

Proceeding further:

Yāvadeva ñāṇamattāya paṭissatimattāya...

Matta means "mere." There is mere wisdom, mere knowledge, mere observation. This is to the extent *(yāvadeva)* that there is no wise person, no one to know or experience. In another Indian tradition it is called *kevalañāṇa kevaladassana,* "only knowing, only seeing."

In the Buddha's time a very old hermit lived at a place called Supārapattaṃ, near present-day Bombay. Having practiced the eight *jhānas,* deep mental absorptions, he thought himself fully enlightened. A well-wisher corrected him, telling him that a Buddha was now present at Sāvatthi, who could teach him the real practice for becoming enlightened. He was so excited to hear this he went all the way to Sāvatthi in northern India. Reaching the monastery, he found that the Buddha had gone out for alms, so he went directly to the city. He found the Buddha walking down a street and immediately understood that this was the Buddha. He asked him then and there for the technique to become an *arahant.* The Buddha told him to wait for an hour or so, to be taught in the monastery, but he insisted: he might die within the hour, or the Buddha might die, or he might lose his present great faith in the Buddha. Now was the time when all these three were present. The Buddha looked and realized that very soon this man would die, and indeed should be given Dhamma now. So he spoke just a few words to this developed old hermit, there on the side of the road: *Diṭṭhe diṭṭhamattaṃ bhavissati...* "In seeing there is mere seeing, in hearing mere hearing, in smelling mere smelling, in tasting mere tasting, in touching mere touching, and in cognizing only cognizing"*...viññāte viññātamattaṃ bhavissati.*

This was sufficient. At the stage of mere knowing, what is being cognized or the identity of who cognizes is irrelevant. There is mere understanding. The dip in *nibbāna* follows, where there is nothing to hold, no base to stand on *(anissito)*.

...anissito ca viharati, na ca kiñci loke upādiyati

The entire field of mind and matter *(loka)* is transcended, and there is no world or universe to grasp *(upādiyati)*.

Whether it is for a few minutes or few hours depends on the capacity and previous work of the person. A person in *nibbāna* is as if dead: none of the senses function, although inside the person is very aware, very alert, very awakened. After that the person returns and again starts functioning in the sensory field, but a fully liberated person has no attachment, no clinging, because there is no craving. Such a person will cling to nothing in the entire universe and nothing clings to them. This is the stage described.

So a meditator practices. Those who practice these sentences will understand the meaning of every word given, but mere intellectualization won't help. Real understanding comes with experience.

Iriyāpathapabbaṃ—Postures of the Body

Iriyāpatha are postures of the body.

gacchanto vā 'gacchāmī' ti pajānāti, ṭhito vā 'ṭhitomhī' ti pajānāti, nisinno vā 'nisinnomhī' ti pajānāti, sayāno vā 'sayānomhī' ti pajānāti.

When walking *(gacchanto)*, a meditator knows well 'I am walking' *('gacchāmi')*. Similarly, whether standing *(ṭhito)*, sitting *(nisinno)*, or lying down *(sayāno)* a meditator knows this well. This is just the beginning. In the sentence that follows, not "I", but just "body" is known well in whatever posture *(yathā yathā paṇihito)*.

Yathā yathā vā panassa kāyo paṇihito hoti, tathā tathā naṃ pajānāti.

Then, in a repetition of the same sentences, the body is observed inside, outside, and both inside and outside simultaneously. Arising is observed, then passing, then both together. Actually it is the sensations that are observed as arising and passing away, because *sampajañña*, the understanding of *anicca*, has to be present, as in every chapter. Awareness follows that 'This is body,' and that it is not "I." This is established with wisdom. Then mere understanding and awareness follow, without any base to hold. There is nothing to grasp.

Iti ajjhattaṃ vā kāye kāyānupassī viharati...'atthi kayo' ti...na ca kiñci loke upādiyati.

Sampajānapabbaṃ— Constant Thorough Understanding of Impermanence

...Abhikkante paṭikkante sampajāna-kārī hoti. Ālokite vilokite... samiñjite pasārite... saṅghāṭi-patta-cīvara-dhāraṇe... asite pīte khāyite sāyite... uccāra-passāva-kamme... gate ṭhite nisinne sutte jāgarite bhāsite tuṇhī-bhāve sampajāna-kārī hoti.

"Walking forward or coming back, looking straight or sideways, bending or stretching, with robes or begging bowl, eating, drinking, chewing, attending to the calls of nature, walking, standing, sitting, lying down, awake or asleep, speaking or remaining silent"—whatever the activity *sampajañña* is being practiced *(sampajāna-kārī hoti)*.

The same stages are then repeated:

> *Iti ajjhattaṃ vā kāye kāyānupassī viharati...'atthi kayo' ti...na ca kiñci loke upādiyati.*

We have already seen that *sampajañña* has to be present everywhere, every moment. The Buddha was frequently asked about *sati*. Every time his reply included *sampajañña*:

> *kāye kāyānupassī viharati ātāpī sampajāno satimā*
> *vedanāsu vedanānupassī viharati ātāpī sampajāno satimā*
> *citte cittānupassī viharati ātāpī sampajāno satimā*
> *dhammesu dhammānupassī viharati ātāpī sampajāno satimā.*

Without *sampajañña*, *sati* is only the awareness of the circus girl. If there is no awareness of arising and passing, it will not lead to liberation.

When asked about *sampajañña* itself, the Buddha used to reply with either of two explanations.

One explanation was the observation with *paññā* of the arising, staying and passing away of three things: *vedanā* (sensation), *saññā* (perception) and *vitakka* (the sense object)—for instance a sound at the ear sense door. These objects are also called *dhammā*, and they flow with sensations—*vedanā-samosaraṇā sabbe dhammā.* Again, the arising and passing of sensation is predominant in *sampajañña.*

The paragraph in this Sutta was another explanation: *sampajañña* embraces every activity. The meaning is that continuity is required.

To illustrate the point, in another discourse the Buddha said:

> *Yato ca bhikkhu ātāpī, sampajaññaṃ na riñcati;*
> *tato so vedanā sabbā parijānāti paṇḍito.*

So vedanā pariññāya diṭṭhe dhamme anāsavo,
kāyassa bhedā Dhammaṭṭho, saṅkhyaṃ nopeti vedagū.

When a meditator practicing ardently,
does not miss *sampajañña* even for a moment,
such a wise one fully understands all sensations.
And having completely understood them, he becomes freed from all impurities.
On the breaking up of the body, such a person, being established in Dhamma and understanding sensations perfectly, attains the indescribable stage beyond the conditioned world.

The *arahant,* having understood the entire field of sensations, from the grossest to the subtlest, does not after death return to this field of arising and passing away. *Sampajañña* is therefore essential in the Buddha's teaching. If you don't understand it you may be carried away in the wrong direction.

Sometimes translations of words create difficulties. Other schools are not to be condemned but we should understand what we are doing. Sometimes *sampajañña* is mistranslated "clear comprehension." Of what? It is taken to mean of gross details: while walking someone comprehends the lifting, moving, placing of one leg, then the other leg, and so forth. Actually the Buddha wants you to feel *vedanā,* arising, staying and passing away. If the understanding of *vedanā* is missed, the whole technique becomes polluted.

Therefore *sampajañña* has to be continuous in every situation. Even when sleeping, it should be present. When students begin they are told that they are helpless in deep sleep, and just to be aware in the waking hours, but at a high stage in meditation there is no normal sleep at all. Full rest is taken, but with *sampajañña* inside, the awareness of sensations arising and passing, of *anicca.* Sometimes on courses students start to have this experience, reporting that they had little or no sleep, but still felt quite fresh. They were with *sampajañña.*

In every chapter the repetition of certain words indicates the importance of this *sampajañña*. *Ātāpī sampajāno satimā* applies to the observation of *kāya, vedanā, citta* and *dhammā*: *sampajañña* has to be present. Similarly *samudaya-, vaya-,* and *samudaya-vaya-dhammānupassī,* which apply everywhere in the *Sutta*, have to be with *sampajañña* and sensations. For example, in Burma there are many pagodas on plateaus, with four staircases, one each from the east, west, north and south. Similarly you might start with *kāya, vedanā, citta,* or *dhammā,* but as you enter the gallery they all intermingle in *vedanā*, and reaching the shrine room it is the same *nibbāna*. Whichever staircase you start climbing, you come to *vedanā* and *sampajañña:* and if you are with *sampajañña* you are progressing step by step towards the final goal.

Make use of the time. You have to work, no one else can work for you. *Pariyatti* will give you proper direction and inspiration, but the benefit will be from your own work. Your practice of *paṭipatti* and *paṭivedhana* is to pierce this curtain of ignorance and reach the ultimate truth about mind, matter and the mental contents, to experience *nibbāna*. Make best use of this opportunity and the facilities. Make use of this wonderful Dhamma for your own good, benefit and liberation from the miseries and bondages of life. May you all enjoy real peace, harmony, and happiness.

May all beings be happy.

DAY FOUR

THE FOURTH DAY of the *Satipaṭṭhāna* course is over. We continue to recite the *Sutta* and to try to understand it in relation to the practice.

We are still in *kāyānupassanā*. You can start with any of the four fields of *kāyānupassanā, vedanānupassanā, cittānupassanā,* or *dhammānupassanā* and with any section of *kāyānupassanā*, but as you proceed they intermingle. You have to reach certain important stations. You have to feel the body inside *(ajjhattaṃ)* and outside *(bahiddhā)*, then both inside and outside *(ajjhatta-bahiddhā)*. You have to experience arising and passing *(samudaya-dhammānupassī viharati, vaya-dhammānupassī viharati)* then both together, *(samudaya-vaya-dhammānupassī viharati)*. You have to feel the entire body as a mass of vibrations arising and passing with great rapidity, in the stage of *bhaṅga*. Then you reach the stage of body as just body *('Atthi kāyo' ti)*, or sensations as just sensations, mind as just mind, or mental contents as just mental contents. There is no identification with it. Then there is the stage of mere awareness *(paṭissati-mattāya)* and mere understanding *(ñāṇa-mattāya)* without any evaluation or reaction.

As you progress and get established in the practice, deep-rooted *saṅkhāras* come on the surface and are eradicated, provided you are *vineyya loke abhijhā-domanassaṃ*, keeping away from craving and aversion towards mind and matter.

In another discourse, the Buddha gave an illustration:

Sabba kamma jahassa bhikkhuno,
dhunamānassa pure kataṃ rajaṃ.

> The meditator who does not make new *kamma*,
> combs out old defilements as they arise.

When a meditator stops generating all *kamma saṅkhāras*, (that is, new actions or reactions), the old impurities—*pure kataṃ rajaṃ*—are combed out. *Dhunamānassa* means combing or carding cotton, separating every fiber, clearing out all the knots and dirt. This can happen at any stage, whenever you don't generate a new *saṅkhāra*, but the very deep-rooted impurities only start coming up after *bhaṅga*. If you keep generating *saṅkhāras*, you keep multiplying your old stock. As long as you refrain from generating any new ones and remain equanimous, layers after layers of *saṅkhāras* are eradicated.

Dhamma is very kind. Initially very crude *saṅkhāras* which would result in a very miserable, low order of new life, surface and get eradicated. You are relieved of them:

> *uppajjitvā nirujjhanti, tesaṃ vūpasamo sukho*

> having arisen, when they are extinguished,
> their eradication brings happiness.

When all the *saṅkhāras* which would have taken you to a lower field of life are gone, the mind becomes perfectly balanced—fit to transcend the field of mind and matter and gain the first glimpse of *nibbāna*.

This may be for a few moments, seconds or minutes, but on returning to the field of mind and matter the meditator's behavior pattern is totally changed. A *saṅkhāra* of the lower fields cannot now be generated. The clan is changed—*gotrabhū*. The *anariyo* becomes a *sotāpanna, ariyo*. Today the word 'aryan' has lost its meaning and is used for a certain race. In the Buddha's day *ariyo* meant a noble person, one who had experienced *nibbāna*. *Sotāpanna* means one who has fallen into the stream, *sota*. Within seven lives at most such a person is bound to keep working to become an *arahant*. No power on earth can stop the process.

The work continues in the same way: *ātāpī sampajāno satimā*. Further deep *saṅkhāras* come on the surface and pass away *(uppajjitvā nirujjhanti)* and a much deeper experience of *nibbāna* results. The meditator returns again to the field of arising and passing, a totally changed person, the stage of *sakadāgāmī* has been reached. Only one more life is possible in the sensual world. Then again the practice is *ātāpī sampajāno satimā*. Finer impurities, but ones which would still give lives of misery, are now eradicated by this equanimity, and the dip in *nibbāna* is again much deeper. The stage of *anāgāmī* is experienced. Now the only possible life is not in the sensual field, but in a very high *Brāhmic* plane. As the meditator continues, the finest *saṅkhāras*—which would give even one life of misery, because they are still within the circle of life and death—are eradicated, and the *nibbāna* of an *arahant* is experienced, total liberation. It can be in this very life or in future lives, but the practice is the same: *ātāpī sampajāno satimā*.

Satimā is with awareness. *Sampajāno* is with wisdom, *paññā*, of arising and passing, direct experience of bodily sensations. Body alone cannot feel sensations and so mind is involved, but in the body is where they are felt. The Buddha gave an illustration: just as different kinds of winds arise in the sky—warm or cold, fast or slow, dirty or clean—so in the body different kinds of sensations arise and pass away.

In another discourse he said:

> *Yato ca bhikkhu ātāpī sampajaññaṃ na rincati,*
> *tato so vedanā sabbā parijānāti paṇḍito.*
>
> Working ardently, without missing *sampajaññaṃ*,
> a meditator experiences the entire field of *vedanā* and gains wisdom.

There are different kinds of *vedanā* whether the *saṅkhāras* are gross, finer or finest. *Sampajaññaṃ* day and night is thus the essence of the whole technique.

So vedanā pariññāya diṭṭhe dhamme anāsavo,
kāyassa bhedā dhammaṭṭho saṅkhyaṃ nopeti vedagū.

"When the entire field of *vedanā* is transcended, Dhamma is understood. Such a person, without impurities *(anāsavā)* fully established in Dhamma *(dhammaṭṭho)* knows perfectly the entire field of sensations *(vedagu)* and does not after death *(kāyassa bhedā)* return to this field of sensations."

This summarizes the whole path to liberation. It is achieved with *sampajañña,* the wisdom of arising and passing, equanimity with sensations. *Ātāpī,* working hard, and *satimā,* when it is the awareness of the circus girl, will not alone liberate because *sampajāñña* is essential.

✧

It is not necessary to pass through every section of *kāyānupassanā*, because each is complete in itself. Only the starting point differs. You can start with any section and reach the same stations and ultimately the final goal. We start with *Ānāpāna,* and later switch to *vedanānupassanā.* However *sampajañña* is required at every stage. The second and third sections of *kāyānupassanā* are always necessary. We practice in the sitting posture, but at times during the day other postures are necessary. The second section covers all four postures of the body (sitting, standing, lying down, and walking) but it still involves *ātāpī sampajāno satimā,* whatever the position or posture. Then the third section involves *sampajañña* continuously in every physical activity. This is necessary because *sampajañña* must always be present. Thus the first three sections on bodily activities must continue throughout our practice, but not every section of *kāyānupassanā.*

Paṭikūlamanasikārapabbaṃ—
Reflections on Repulsiveness

Paṭikūla means "repulsive." *Manasikāra* means "reflection" or "contemplation." This will not in itself take you to the final goal. The Buddha teaches direct experience, not mere imagination or intellectualization. However in some cases, when the mind is very dull or agitated, it cannot start with respiration, let alone with equanimity with the feeling of sensations. In most cases such people have strong attachment to the body and are engrossed in sexual pleasures, obsessed by the outer beauty of the body. They won't try to understand, and cannot practice Dhamma, so this contemplation of repulsiveness is used to balance the mind at least slightly. They are asked just to start thinking in the proper way: what is this body?

> *imameva kāyaṃ uddhaṃ pādatalā adho kesamatthhakā tacapariyantaṃ pūraṃ nānappakārassa asucino paccavekkhati...*

From the soles of the feet up and from the hairs of the head down the entire body covered by skin is reflected on or thought about *(paccavekkhati)* as impure *(asucino)* in different ways *(nānappakārassa)*. It is all so ugly. It contains hair of the head, hair of the body, nails, teeth, skin, flesh, sinews, bones, marrow, kidney, heart, liver, pleura, spleen, lungs, intestines, mesentery, stomach and contents, feces, bile, phlegm, pus, blood, sweat, fat, tears, grease, saliva, nasal mucus, synovial fluid, and urine. This is its nature.

This is just a beginning for those not in a position to observe reality inside. Impurity keeps overpowering them. Once they can think properly, they are fit to practice, either with respiration or directly with sensations. Of course, when the actual practice of Vipassana starts, there should be no aversion towards this ugly body. It is just observed as it is—*yathābhūta*. It is observed as body, with sensations arising and passing. The meditator is now on the path.

The Buddha gives an example of a double-mouthed provision bag full of different seeds and grains, such as hill paddy, paddy, green gram, cowpeas, sesame and husked rice. Just as a man with good eyes can see all these different grains, so such things are seen in this body covered with skin. When divine eye is developed, at a much later stage, it becomes very easy to see the body. Every part—indeed, every particle of the body—is seen as if with open eyes.

> *Iti ajjhattaṃ vā kāye kāyānupassī viharati…'atthi kayo' ti…na ca kiñci loke upādiyati.*

Then the process is the same. Although the starting point varies according to the background and mental capacity of the person, the ending stations are the same. The body is observed inside and out, *ajjhatta-bahiddhā.* The arising and passing away is observed: *samudaya-vaya.* Then *'Atthi kāyo' ti,* "This is body." The awareness gets established, and without any support in this world of mind and matter, there is nothing to grasp *(na ca kiñci loke upādiyati)* in the stage of full liberation.

Dhātumanasikārapabbaṃ—
Reflections on Material Elements

Dhātu means element. Again, for a certain type of person with strong attachment to the body and to sexual pleasures, thinking is involved at the beginning of the practice.

> *imameva kāyaṃ yathāṭhitaṃ yathāpaṇihitaṃ dhātuso paccavekkhati: 'Atthi imasmiṃ kāye pathavīdhātu āpodhātu tejodhātu vāyodhātū' ti.*

However the body is placed or disposed *(kayaṃ yathāṭhitaṃ yathāpaṇihitaṃ)*, the elements in it are just thought about *(paccavekkhati)*: earth *(pathavī)*, water *(āpo)*, fire *(tejo)*, and air *(vāyo)*.

The Buddha gives another example. Just as a butcher or his apprentice kills a cow, divides it into portions bit by bit, and sells it seated in the marketplace, so the body is understood as being just these four elements. It consists of: solidity—flesh, bones, and so forth; liquidity—blood, urine, and so forth; gases; and temperature. Just as "cow" is a conventional word for a composition of parts, so the body is nothing else but these four elements, none of which is "body." Thus people are brought to the point where the mind is at least slightly balanced.

Iti ajjhattaṃ vā kāye kāyānupassī viharati... 'atthi kāyo' ti... na ca kiñci loke upādiyati.

Then the same work starts, because mere thinking is not sufficient. The same stations have to be passed through. The stage is reached of *Atthi kāyo' ti,* "This is body," to which there was formerly so much attachment, and putting aside all attachments the meditator reaches the final goal.

Navasivathikapabbaṃ— Nine Cemetery Observations

There were some people, then as now, with so much attachment to the body that even proper thinking was impossible. Therefore a cruder, grosser starting point was given: they were just taken to a cemetery. This was of the kind where the dead body is not burned or buried, but just thrown away to be eaten by birds, animals, and so forth. Unable to work with their attention inside themselves, they were just asked to start looking at a corpse. Then they could consider their own body in the same way:

So imameva kāyaṃ upasaṃharati: 'ayaṃ pi kho kāyo evaṃdhammo evaṃbhāvī evaṃanatīto' ti.

They think *(upasaṃharati)* about their own body: "My body too is of the same nature, it will unavoidably become like this." There are nine cemetery contemplations:

> They view a corpse that is one day, two days, or three days old, swollen, blue, and festering. They consider and understand that their body also has the same nature, and will ultimately die with the same result.

Again they view a corpse thrown in a cemetery being eaten by crows, hawks, vultures, dogs, jackals, or different kinds of worms. Again they consider their own body in the same way.

They view a corpse reduced to a skeleton with flesh or blood attached, held together by tendons. Then they consider their own body.

They view a corpse reduced to a skeleton without any flesh but smeared with blood and held together by tendons.

They view a corpse reduced to a skeleton without flesh or blood attached, held together by tendons.

This time they view only disconnected bones scattered in all directions: the bone of a hand or foot, a knee bone, thigh bone, pelvis, spine, or skull.

Now after a long time the bones are white, bleached.

They view bones that, after more than a year are just lying in a heap.

They view bones that are rotting and breaking down into dust.

Each time, after viewing, they reflect in the same way about their own body.

It is necessary to begin with just viewing in this way because Vipassana—to observe and experience the true nature of reality—is a delicate job. People living a coarse, gross life, involved in gross impurities, cannot do it. Special cases are therefore taken to a cemetery, just to see, to keep contemplating, and to understand what they see as the ultimate result for everyone. They are asked to start thinking. With this feeling of repulsiveness and now with understanding, the mind is slightly balanced: it can practice.

Iti ajjhattaṃ vā kāye kāyānupassī viharati... 'atthi kāyo' ti... na ca kiñci loke upādiyati.

Now they start working through the same stations. They reach the stage of *'atthi kāyo' ti,* "This is body," to which there was so much attachment. Then they continue until all attachments are given up at the stage of full liberation.

✧

The path is the same in every section. Only the starting point differs. In every section you must feel arising and passing away, manifesting as sensation, which is the combination of mind and matter. First you feel it separately, then together when it arises and instantly passes away. Then everywhere the entire structure is dissolved, arising, passing, arising, passing. You just observe. In this way you develop your faculties of *sati* and *sampajañña*—the wisdom that develops equanimity.

There can be a type of equanimity even without the understanding of *anicca.* It is achieved by repeatedly suggesting nonreaction and calmness to the mind. Many people develop this faculty and seem not to react or be upset by the vicissitudes of life. They are balanced, but only at the surface level. A deeper part of the mind keeps on reacting because it is in constant contact with bodily sensations at a depth they have not reached. Without *sampajañña*, the roots of the behavior pattern of reaction—the *saṅkhāras*—remain.

This is why the Buddha gave so much importance to *vedanā.* To put aside craving and aversion is a traditional teaching of the past. In India there were teachers before and after the Buddha, and teachers contemporary to the Buddha, who taught it, and whose disciples practiced it. Yet it was only in relation to outside objects: that which was seen, heard, smelt, tasted, touched, or thought. The Buddha went deeper. Both the six sense doors and their objects were called *saḷāyatana.* He discovered that the contact between the two inevitably results in sensation, and that craving or aversion arises only after the sensation arises.

Saḷāyatana paccayā phasso,
phassā paccayā vedanā,
vedanā paccayā taṇhā:

Contact is because of the sense doors, sensation is because of contact, craving is because of sensation. This was his enlightenment.

The gap, the missing link, was *vedanā.* Without it people were dealing only with the sense objects, and their reactions to these objects. They could only rectify the intellect, the surface of the mind. Yet at the deepest level, following the contact, part of the mind evaluates this contact as good or bad. This evaluation gives a pleasant or unpleasant sensation. Then the reaction of craving or aversion starts. From his own experience the Buddha continued to teach equanimity towards sensations, to change the behavior pattern of the mind at the deepest level, and to come out of bondage.

This is what you have started practicing. You are developing equanimity not merely to the sense objects—sound, vision, smell, taste, touch or thought—but to the sensations that you feel, pleasant, unpleasant or neutral. *Sampajañña* has started with the understanding of the characteristic of arising and passing in bodily sensations. Having worked with *Ānāpāna* you easily experience sensations and you are developing equanimity with this understanding. You are practicing the Buddha's exact words. You work hard to remain *satimā* and *sampajāno: ātāpī sampajāno satimā.* This is the message of the whole *Satipaṭṭhāna Sutta.*

Make use of whatever time is left on this serious course. Reading and understanding the *Sutta* at the intellectual level will give much inspiration, guidance and confidence that you are doing what the Buddha intended: but intellectual understanding will not in itself liberate you. Make use of this *Sutta* and these evening discourses, but work. Work day and night, *sampajaññaṃ na rincati.* In deep sleep you are helpless, but otherwise you should not miss *sampajañña* for a moment, whatever you are doing—eating, drinking, walking, or lying down. Of course, at this stage the mind still wanders and you forget. You start contemplating, imagining or thinking, but see how quickly you realize, and start again with sensations. Keep reminding yourself. Develop your wisdom, your enlightenment. You have to change the old habit pattern of running away from sensations; you must remain with the deeper reality of arising and passing, *samudaya-vaya, anicca.* Come out of the ignorance, the bondage. Make use of these wonderful days of your life to come out of all your miseries. May you all enjoy real peace, real harmony, real happiness.

May all beings be happy.

DAY FIVE

THE FIFTH DAY of the *Satipaṭṭhāna* course is over. We have covered *kāyānupassanā.*

Kāyānupassanā is not complete without *vedanānupassanā,* because *anupassanā* means to continuously experience the truth, which means to feel the body. Actually *vedanā* is central in all four *satipaṭṭhānas.* Mind and mental contents also have to be felt. Without feeling, the practice is just an intellectual game. This tradition emphasizes *vedanā* because it gives us a tangible understanding of *anicca,* of arising and passing, *samudaya, vaya.* This understanding at the level of *vedanā* is absolutely essential because without it there is no *sampajañña.* Without *sampajañña* there is no *paññā.* Without *paññā* there is no Vipassana. Without Vipassana there is no *Satipaṭṭhāna,* and no liberation.

Deep *samādhi* can be gained using any object of concentration. For instance the breath coming and going, as in the first paragraph of the *Ānāpāna* section, can be used to gain the deep absorption of the first *jhāna,* then the deeper absorption of the second *jhāna* and then the third and fourth *jhānas.* It is quite possible that along with the awareness of respiration, sensation may also be felt; but without the appreciation of arising and passing, it is not Vipassana. Then from the fifth to the eighth *jhānas* the body is forgotten. These work with the mind only, and imagination is used.

Before his enlightenment, the Buddha had already learnt the seventh and eighth *jhānas* from Āḷāra Kālāma and Uddaka Rāmaputta, and certainly attained much purification. However he still found deep-rooted impurities inside, which he called *anusaya kilesa. Saya* means sleeping. *Anu* indicates that they follow with the mind from birth to birth. Like dormant volcanoes they can erupt at any time, and one of them always arises at the time of death. The others just follow on to the next life. For this reason, though he had perfected the eight *jhānas,* he did not accept himself as liberated.

Bodily torture also produced no result. He continued to investigate. From respiration he started observing sensation, and from this he gained the understanding of arising and passing. The key to liberation was found. The *jhānas* which he had practiced previously now had Vipassana, *sampajañña,* added to them. Previously they were called *lokiya jhānas* because they still resulted in new birth and so rotation in the *loka*, the planes of the universe. Now they were called *lokuttara jhānas,* because with the experience of arising and passing they gave the fruit of *nibbāna,* beyond the *loka.* This is the Buddha's contribution to humankind, and it is attained with *vedanā,* which is why *vedanā* is so important for us.

Vedanānupassanā— Observation of Sensations

vedanāsu vedanānupassī viharati

How are sensations observed in sensations? No imagination is involved. It is not as if the meditator is outside and thus examining his or her feelings. No one is standing outside. You must have direct experience. The same applies to *kāya,* and later to *citta* and *dhammā.* The observation must be without any separation of observer and observed, or the imagination of any outside examiner.

...sukhaṃ vā vedanaṃ vedayamāno 'sukhaṃ vedanaṃ vedayāmī' ti pajānāti...

Experiencing a pleasant sensation *(sukhaṃ vedanaṃ vedayamāno)* the meditator understands this as the experience of a pleasant sensation.

...dukkhaṃ vā vedanaṃ vedayamāno 'dukkhaṃ vedanaṃ vedayāmī' ti pajānāti; adukkhamasukhaṃ vā vedanaṃ vedayamāno 'adukkhamasukhaṃ vedanaṃ vedayāmī' ti pajānāti.

The same applies to unpleasant *(dukkha vedana)* sensation, such as pain; and neutral sensation *(adukkhamasukha vedana)*, which is neither pleasant nor unpleasant. The words *sukha* and *dukkha* refer to bodily feelings. For pleasant or unpleasant mental feelings, the Buddha used *somanassa* and *domanassa. Sukha* and *dukkha vedanā* therefore refer to sensation on the body. Body by itself cannot feel them, and they are felt by a part of the mind; nevertheless the body is the base.

Sāmisaṃ vā sukhaṃ vedanaṃ vedayamāno 'sāmisaṃ sukhaṃ vedanaṃ vedayāmī' ti pajānāti; nirāmisaṃ vā sukhaṃ vedanaṃ vedayamāno 'nirāmisaṃ sukhaṃ vedanaṃ vedayāmī' ti pajānāti.

A pleasant sensation is understood properly as being with craving or attachment *(sāmisa)* or without craving or attachment *(nirāmisa)*. In today's India *nirāmisa* means vegetarian and *sāmisa* means nonvegetarian food. The meaning here is pure or impure. A pleasant sensation arising as result of proper Vipassana meditation, if it is observed without craving or attachment, leads to purity. The same pleasant sensation, perhaps encountered through involvement in some sensual pleasure, if it is reacted to with craving and attachment, with an attempt to increase it, is unwholesome and leads to impurity. It leads to rotation in misery. In this sense, a pleasant sensation may be pure or impure.

A *sāmisa* sensation is just to be observed, so that the reaction weakens and stops. A *nirāmisa* sensation, towards which there is equanimity, and no reaction, is also just observed. Then naturally according to the law, this faculty of objective observation increases. You do nothing. *Pajānāti* is mere observation, based in wisdom.

Sāmisaṃ vā dukkhaṃ vedanaṃ... nirāmisaṃ vā dukkhaṃ vedanaṃ... pajānāti.

Sāmisaṃ vā adukkhamasukhaṃ vedanaṃ... nirāmisaṃ vā adukkhamasukhaṃ vedanaṃ vedayamāno 'nirāmisaṃ adukkhamasukhaṃ vedanaṃ vedayāmī' ti pajānāti.

Similarly whether the unpleasant *(dukkha)* sensation experienced is pure or impure depends on whether there is a reaction to it. It also is just observed, understood and accepted as it is. The neutral *(adukkhamasukha)* sensation is understood in the same way.

Iti ajjhattaṃ vā vedanāsu vedanānupassī viharati, bahiddhā vā vedanāsu vedanānupassī viharati, ajjhattabahiddhā vā vedanāsu vedanānupassī viharati.

As in every section, similar stations now follow. The sensations are felt inside and on the surface of the body, and then simultaneously throughout the entire physical structure.

Another tradition interprets *ajjhattaṃ* as the feeling on one's own body, *bahiddhā* as the feeling on someone else's body, and *ajjhatta-bahiddhā* as switching between the two. As before, our tradition does not accept this. The meditator is working alone, whether in the forest, under a tree, or in a cell. It is argued that when begging for food the monk encounters others and has this opportunity to feel their breath or sensations. However the eyes of serious meditators are downcast *(okkhitta-cakkhu)* and at most they might see someone else's legs as they walk: so this interpretation seems illogical. Of course, at a very high stage of observation the meditator becomes very sensitive to the sensations of others also, and to the vibrations of the surrounding atmosphere and of animate and inanimate objects. Possibly it could be understood in this way. Otherwise to practice on someone else's breath or sensations is unworkable. It is better therefore to take *ajjhattaṃ* as "inside" and *bahiddhā* as "on the surface of one's own body."

...samudayadhammānupassī... vayadhammānupassī... samudayavayadhammānupassī vā vedanāsu viharati...

This and the following stations, which occur in every section, are very important. The meditator has to pass through them. The arising of *vedanā,* the passing of *vedanā,* and the arising and instant passing of *vedanā* are felt.

...'atthi vedanā' ti vā panassa sati paccupaṭṭhitā hoti.

In *kāyānupassanā* the stage of *'atthi kāyo' ti* came when the body became merely a mass of subatomic particles, with no valuation or judgement: *saññā* no longer recognized it as human or animal, male or female, beautiful or ugly. It became just body as body, beyond differentiation. Similarly sensations, *vedanā,* are now seen just as sensations, *vedanā,* neither pleasant nor unpleasant. There is no judgement, no evaluation, no *saññā.* The awareness now established is of sensations as just sensations. Then the same stations follow to the final goal.

Yāvadeva ñāṇamattāya paṭissatimattāya anissito ca viharati, na ca kiñci loke upādiyati.

The role of *vedanā* was the Buddha's great discovery for humanity. It is the important junction from which two roads start: either *dukkha-samudaya-gāminī paṭipadā,* the road in which misery is continuously generated, or *dukkha-nirodha-gāminī paṭipadā,* the road in which misery becomes totally eradicated. He discovered that every reaction, every *saṅkhāra* can be generated only with the feeling of sensation—pleasant, unpleasant or neutral. At the deepest level the mind constantly reacts to *vedanā* throughout the body, in every particle, all the time, wherever there is life. Unless sensations, *vedanā*, are experienced, any freedom from craving or aversion is only at the surface of the mind. It is an illusion of nonreaction because it is only in relation to outside objects: to the outside world of sound, vision, smell, touch—feeling or taste. What is missed is the reality of your reaction because every contact of an object with a sense door is bound to produce a sensation on the body, pleasant, unpleasant or neutral. This is missed.

You must go to that depth where you feel sensations and yet do not react. Only when you are aware of sensations and equanimous towards them can the habit pattern of the mind be changed at the deepest level. Deep-rooted *saṅkhāras* like lines drawn on rock with chisel and hammer—the *anusaya kilesa*—can then come up and pass away. Otherwise the process of multiplication continues. Therefore *vedanā* plays such an important role in *Satipaṭṭhāna.*

Cittānupassanā—Observation of Mind

citte cittānupassī viharati

How does a meditator practice observation of mind in mind?

"*In* mind" *(citte)* means by direct experience, as "*in* body" and "*in* sensations." To avoid any imagination about the mind something must happen in it, because as something happens and then passes away, it can be felt as sensation.

sarāgaṃ vā cittaṃ 'sarāgaṃ cittaṃ' ti pajānāti, vītarāgaṃ vā cittaṃ 'vītarāgaṃ cittaṃ' ti pajānāti.

Sarāgaṃ means with craving, *sa-rāga.* If craving has arisen in the mind, this is just observed. When it passes away, and the mind is free of it *(vīta-rāgaṃ)* this is just observed: the craving arose and passed away.

sadosaṃ vā cittaṃ... vītadosaṃ vā cittaṃ 'vitadosaṃ cittaṃ' ti pajānāti,

samohaṃ vā cittaṃ 'samohaṃ cittaṃ' ti pajānāti, vītamohaṃ vā cittaṃ 'vītamohaṃ cittaṃ' ti pajānāti.

The reality of a mind with or without aversion *(dosa)* is observed and when the aversion passes away the mind is free of it.

Similarly *moha* (illusion, delusion, confusion, ignorance) is observed: when it has gone the mind is free of it.

Saṅkhittaṃ vā cittaṃ ..vikkhittaṃ vā cittaṃ...
mahaggataṃ vā cittaṃ... amahaggataṃ vā cittaṃ...
sa-uttaraṃ vā cittaṃ... anuttaraṃ vā cittaṃ...
samāhitaṃ vā cittaṃ... asamāhitaṃ vā cittaṃ...
vimuttaṃ vā cittaṃ... avimuttaṃ vā cittaṃ 'avimuttaṃ cittaṃ' ti pajānāti.

Whether the mind is collected and concentrated *(saṅkhitta)* or *vikkhitta* (scattered)—this is just observed and accepted. In deeper *jhānas* when the mind is expanded, using imagination, to a limitless area, it is called *mahaggata,* big. Whether or not it is *mahaggata*—this is just observed. *Sa-uttara* means there are higher minds, or scope for development. *Anuttara* is when there is nothing higher: mind has reached the highest stage. This also is observed. Whether the mind is deeply absorbed in *samādhi (samāhita)* or not is observed. Whether the mind is liberated *(vimutta)* or in bondage is also observed.

Iti ajjhattaṃ vā... bahiddhā vā...ajjhattabahiddhā vā citte cittānupassī viharati.

The same stations follow. Mind is observed inside and outside. Again, this tradition does not accept *bahiddhā* as the mind of someone else. At a high stage of purification the meditator does develop the psychic power to read the minds of others, but this is not a final station.

Mind inside *(ajjhattaṃ)* is a mind experiencing something within the framework of the body. Mind is taken as outside when it experiences an object from outside: when it feels a sound coming into contact with the ear, a shape with the eye, a smell with the nose, a taste with the tongue, something tangible with the body, or a thought of something outside. However the whole process is still within the framework of the body. Mind itself always remains inside the body, even when its object is outside.

Then arising and passing is experienced and the stage of *'atthi cittaṃ' ti* is reached: it is just *viññāṇa,* just mind, not "I" or "my" mind. The awareness gets established in this. Then there is mere wisdom or understanding, mere observation. There is nothing to support or to grasp.

'Atthi cittaṃ' ti...na ca kiñci loke upādiyati.

A Vipassana meditator understands how, when there is mere awareness, only cognition *(viññāṇa)* functions. There is no process of multiplication of misery. Recall the words spoken to the old hermit who came all the way from near Bombay to Sāvatthi to meet the Buddha. These words were sufficient, in that the hermit had already practiced eight *jhānas: diṭṭhe diṭṭhamattaṃ bhavissati....* "In seeing there is only seeing," nothing beyond it, because there is no evaluation or reaction. "There is just hearing as hearing, smelling as smelling, tasting as tasting, touching as touching, and *...viññāte viññātamattaṃ* ...cognizing as cognizing." This high stage takes time. But it must be reached to experience *nibbāna.*

The practice is to understand this process. All the sense doors are on the body, so the body is central. There is a contact with the eye, ear, nose, tongue, body touch, or mind. *Viññāṇa* cognizes that something has happened. Then *saññā* evaluates it as good or bad, and the sensation that results is pleasant or unpleasant. *Saṅkhāra* reacts, and bondage, misery starts. These other aggregates overpower *viññāṇa. Saṅkhāra* has become so strong and *viññāṇa* so weak. As a result, misery and bondage have become so strong. The practice is to weaken *saṅkhāra* and *saññā,* and to strengthen *viññāṇa,* until there is nothing else but mere understanding and awareness—*yāvadeva ñāṇamattāya paṭissati-mattāya.*

The Buddha practiced eight *jhānas* before his enlightenment. The name of the eighth *jhāna* is *nevasaññā-*

nāsaññāyatana: in this *jhāna, saññā* cannot be said either to exist or not exist. Although it has become so feeble, it does still exist, so the Buddha did not yet call himself a liberated person. Using Vipassana he developed the *lokuttara jhānas,* leading to *nibbāna,* and introduced the "ninth *jhāna,*" which he called *saññā-vedayita-nirodha:* where *saññā* and *vedanā* stop. So long as *saññā* functions, however feebly, it will produce a reaction, a *saṅkhāra. Sañña* must be totally eradicated to experience the stage of *viññāṇa* as *viññāṇa.*

Dhammānupassanā— Observation of Mental Contents

dhammesu dhammānupassi viharati

Just as *kāyānupassanā* is incomplete without *vedanānupassanā,* so *cittānupassanā* is incomplete without *dhammānupassanā.* For the mind and body be felt, something must arise on them; otherwise the practice is just imagination. Therefore *citta* can only be experienced when something arises and passes away, such as *rāga, dosa,* or *moha.*

What mind contains is called *dhamma.*

Many words used by the Buddha are difficult to translate, because they have no equivalents in other languages. Of these, *dhamma* is the most difficult. Its range of meaning is vast. Its root meaning is *dhāretī' ti dhamma:* that which is contained. It is what is contained in the mind.

A further meaning became the nature or the characteristic of whatever arises in the mind:

> *Attano sabhāvaṃ attano lakkhanaṃ dhāretī' ti dhamma.*
>
> *Dhamma* means the self-nature, the self-characteristic that is contained.

Sometimes in the languages of India today, it is said that the *dhamma* of fire is to burn. Burning is its characteristic, otherwise it is not fire. The *dhamma* of ice is to cool, or it is not ice. Similarly *rāga* (craving) contains its own *dhamma* or characteristic, which is to create agitation and misery. The *dhamma* of love and compassion is calmness, harmony and peace. So *dhamma* became the nature or the quality.

After a few centuries the term *dhamma*, or nature, was divided into *kusala* (wholesome) and *akusala* (unwholesome), referring to its fruit. Impurities contained in the mind—such as anger, hatred, animosity, passion, fear, and ego, which give unwholesome fruit—were called *akusala.* Qualities which were to one's credit and gave a better life—such as compassion, goodwill and selfless service—were called *kusala.* Thus in the old literature we find *dhamma* divided into "pure" and "impure."

Slowly *akusala* became *adhamma* or *pāpa,* anti-Dhamma or sin, that which causes rotation in misery. Then Dhamma became used for anything wholesome, contained in a person, which leads to liberation.

The meaning of *dhamma* continued to expand. As the result of a mental content is observed—say what happens as result of anger or compassion—the law of cause and effect, that is the law of nature, starts to be understood. Therefore *dhamma* can be whatever is contained in the mind, or the characteristic of that which is contained, or the law of nature—that is, the law of the universe.

How does a meditator practice observation of the *dhammas*?

Nīvaraṇapabbaṃ—The Hindrances

dhammesu dhammānupassī viharati pañcasu nīvaraṇesu.

Nīvaraṇa means a "curtain" or "cover": that which prevents the reality from being seen. In the ten-day courses we refer to the *nīvaraṇas* as the five enemies: craving, aversion, drowsiness, agitation, and doubt. An example is given. At that time there were no mirrors, and people used to look at the reflection of their faces in a pot of clean water with a light. If the water is dirty, colored, or agitated, you can't see properly. Similarly, these *nīvaraṇas* are enemies to your progress on the path of observing reality because they color or prevent you from seeing it.

Again there is no imagination involved: *dhamma* is experienced in *dhamma (dhammesu)*. Nor does this section involve any contemplation. How then are these hindrances observed?

> *santaṃ vā ajjhattaṃ kāmacchandaṃ 'atthi me ajjhattaṃ kāmacchando' ti pajānāti,*
>
> *asantaṃ vā ajjhattaṃ kāmacchandaṃ 'natthi me ajjhattaṃ kāmacchando' ti pajānāti*

When a craving for sensual pleasures *(kāmacchanda)* is present inside, this is just accepted. There is just awareness of this fact. When it is not present, this is understood: just awareness of the reality as it is, from moment to moment.

> *...yathā ca anuppannassa kāmacchandassa uppādo hoti taṃ ca pajānāti, yathā ca uppannassa kāmacchandassa pahānaṃ hoti taṃ ca pajānāti, yathā ca pahīnassa kāmacchandassa āyatiṃ anuppādo hoti taṃ ca pajānāti.*

Then those *kāmacchandas* which were lying deep inside and had not previously come to the surface *(anuppanna)* now do so *(uppāda)*. This is also understood *(pajānāti)*. Things arise and sooner or later pass away, *samudayavaya;* similarly this craving arises and passes away. As layers after layers arise and are observed, they are eradicated *(pahāna)*. The layers that have been eradicated *(pahīna)* do not come back again *(āyatiṃ anuppādo)*. All this is just observed and understood *(pajānāti)*.

When all the accumulated craving has been eradicated, full liberation is reached. The mental habit of generating craving is gone, and no such *saṅkhāra* can be generated now.

Santaṃ vā ajjhattaṃ byāpādaṃ...
Santaṃ vā ajjhattaṃ thinamiddhaṃ...
Santaṃ vā ajjhattaṃ uddhaccakukkuccaṃ...
Santaṃ vā ajjhattaṃ vicikicchaṃ... taṃ ca pajānāti.

In the same way the meditator understands aversion *(byāpādaṃ)* to be present or absent. The whole process of Vipassana is described in these paragraphs. Whatever past aversion was lying low, like a dormant volcano deep inside, arises. This is also observed and eradicated. Unless the habit pattern is totally changed, *saṅkhāras* of aversion of the same type will start anew. When all are eradicated at the root level, nothing comes back. This is the final goal. It is impossible for an *arahant* to generate any new craving or aversion.

Similarly *thīna-midda* (drowsiness of the mind and body), *uddhacca-kukkucca* (agitation) and *vicikicchā* (doubts, skepticism) are eradicated.

It should be clear that every *dhamma,* anything that arises on the mind—even a slight thought—starts flowing with a sensation on the body: *vedanā samosaranā sabbe dhammā.* This law of nature was realized but not created by the Buddha. Whatever arises—anger, passion, or anything else—if the sensation is observed the meditator is working properly. Otherwise it is an intellectual game. Anger may have gone away at the surface level, but deep inside the sensation remains, and the mind continues to react with anger to this sensation without the meditator even knowing. Therefore, so far as this tradition is concerned, the sensation on the body cannot be missed. The words of the Buddha are so clear: *sampajaññaṃ na rincati.* Every moment there must be awareness of sensation arising and passing.

Whether you are practicing any section of *kāyānupassanā* or *vedanānupassanā,* or *cittānupassanā* or *dhammānupassanā,* without the understanding of arising and passing of sensation, the accumulated impurities at the depth of the mind can be neither reached nor eradicated. The practice will just be a surface game.

The same stations follow:

Iti ajjhattaṃ vā dhammesu dhammānupassī viharati... 'atthi dhamma' ti...na ca kiñci loke upādiyati.

Observing inside and on the surface, and then arising and passing, the stage of *'atthi dhammā' ti,* is reached: neither good nor bad, mine nor yours, just the law of nature, mere mental contents and their nature. The same stations follow until there is nothing to grasp.

When craving has arisen, you can't take it out with aversion; otherwise you generate a new *saṅkhāra* of aversion. If you just accept that there is craving in the mind, then you are just observing, and the reaction, which is the nature of craving, is not being multiplied. It is weakened and becomes feeble. Any mental impurity is similarly observed. Even the practice of intellectually contemplating the body as repulsive, as in some opening paragraphs of *kāyānupassanā,* was given by the Buddha merely as a beginning to bring people on the right path. Once Vipassana starts, there is no aversion to this ugly body; it is just observed as it is with the wisdom of arising and passing—*yathābhūta-ñāṇa-dassanaṃ.* The *ñāṇa,* as in *pajānāti,* is just awareness with the understanding of *anicca.* Whatever arises—whether good or bad, pure or impure—there is mere observation, no attempt to retain or push it out. This is the proper path to the final goal.

The path is long, but it starts with the first step. Don't be disheartened if the final goal is far away. No effort is wasted on this path. Whatever effort you make gives you benefit. You have started on the right path to the final goal. Step by step, as you come nearer and nearer, you are bound to reach the final goal.

May all of you keep walking on this path, step by step. Make use of the time and the facility. Understanding the direct words of the Buddha, make use of this wonderful technique. As much as possible try not to miss *sampajañña* in any situation. Excepting only the time of deep sleep, try to be aware with *sampajañña* in every physical activity, for your own good, benefit and liberation. May you all be liberated from the bondages, the miseries.

May all beings be happy.

DAY SIX

THE SIXTH DAY of the *Satipaṭṭhāna* course is over. We proceed further with *Dhammānupassanā. Dhammas* are mental contents and their nature, the universal law of nature. A Buddha, an enlightened person, has no interest in establishing a sect or religion. Having discovered ultimate truth at the deepest level, the Buddha teaches this law to help people understand reality and end their misery, whatever their sect, community, country, color or gender. The entire universe, animate and inanimate, everyone and everything, is governed by this law. With or without the Buddha, it governs the constant interaction of mind and matter, the currents, undercurrents and cross-currents going on in each individual. Yet people keep on playing games at the surface of the mind, deluding themselves in ignorance and multiplying their misery by multiplying their bondages.

Khandhapabbaṃ—The Aggregates

> *dhammesu dhammānupassī viharati pañcasu upādānakkhandhesu*

Khandha means an aggregate, an accumulation, or a heap of something. We are called individual beings. This is an apparent truth: but at a deeper level every living individual—I, you, he, or she—is just *pañca khandhā,* the five aggregates. The Buddha wants you to go to the depth of this reality, where you cannot differentiate or identify by name, where they are merely the five aggregates.

One aggregate is the countless, subatomic material particles, *kalāpas,* joined together as matter. Mind is divided into another four aggregates: *viññāṇa* cognizes; *saññā* recognizes and evaluates; *vedanā* feels; and *saṅkhāra* reacts and creates. These five aggregates combined are called an entity, an individual. At the ultimate level they are just five aggregates and the whole process of *Satipaṭṭhāna,* of Vipassana, is to experience this fact. Otherwise the delusion of identifying "I," "mine," or "myself" with any or all of these aggregates—which is ignorance—causes tremendous attachment and clinging to them, resulting in great misery. This is not a belief to be accepted out of devotion, just because an enlightened person said it, nor a philosophy just to be intellectually accepted as rational and logical. It is a truth to be experienced and realized at the actual level within the framework of the body. When this truth becomes clear, the habit pattern at the deepest level of the mind changes, and liberation is reached. This is Dhamma, the law.

Upādāna means attachment and clinging. This develops towards the five aggregates, which are its object; or, the five aggregates are generated and come together because of *upādāna.* They are aggregates of attachment.

Again a meditator observes *dhamma* in *dhamma,* the five aggregates. How does a meditator practice with them?

> *...'iti rūpaṃ, iti rūpassa samudayo, iti rūpassa atthaṅgamo...*

This is matter, this is the arising of matter, this is the passing away of matter: all this is experienced. *Rūpa* means matter, *samudaya* means arising, *atthaṅgamo* passing away.

> *iti vedanā, iti vedanāya samudayo, iti vedanāya atthaṅgamo;*
>
> *iti saññā, iti saññāya samudayo, iti saññāya atthaṅgamo;*
> *iti saṅkhārā, iti saṅkhārānaṃ samudayo, iti saṅkhārānaṃ atthaṅgamo;*
> *iti viññāṇaṃ, iti viññāṇassa samudayo, iti viññāṇassa atthaṅgamo' ti.*

As the mental aggregates also are experienced—sensation *(vedana)*, perception *(sañña)*, reaction *(saṅkhāra)*, and consciousness *(viññāṇa)*—the whole process of what is happening inside is realized.

Iti ajjhattaṃ vā dhammesu dhammānupassī viharati,...'atthi dhamma' ti....

The same stations follow, inside, outside, both together. Then *"atthi dhammā ti,"*—"Oh, this is Dhamma." Awareness gets established in the reality that these five aggregates are all there is. A high stage of observation finds mere mind and matter, nothing else—no "I," "mine," or "myself."

At the apparent, conventional level, the words "I" and "you" have to be used, but at the actual, ultimate level there are just the five *khandhas.* Similarly for conventional purposes, we call something joined together a motor car, but if we disintegrate it and separate its parts, which part is the car? the tires? the wheels? the seats? the engine? the battery? the body? Actually a car is just different parts joined together.

Similarly, Monday, Tuesday, Wednesday, Thursday, Friday, Saturday and Sunday when joined make a week; thirty days joined together make a month; and twelve months a year, for conventional purposes only. Vipassana divides, dissects, disintegrates and observes reality as it is. Then the attachment goes away. The *khandhās* remain, arising and passing, but they are mere aggregates, because *upādāna* is gone. This is the Dhamma of the *khandhās.*

Yāvadeva ñāṇamattāya paṭissatimattāya anissito ca viharati, na ca kiñci loke upādiyati.

Then comes *ñāṇamattāya paṭissatimattāya* also known in those days as *samyak darshana, kevala darshana, samyak jñāna kevala jñāna*—mere observation and mere understanding. Then *anissito ca viharati:* there is nothing to depend on because there is no attachment; there is nothing to grasp.

Āyatanapabbaṃ—The Sense Spheres

> *dhammesu dhammānupassī viharati chasu ajjhattikabāhiresu āyatanesu.*

The *āyatanas* are the six sense spheres or doors: the eyes, ears, nose, tongue, body, and mind. All six are inside *(ajjhattika)* because they are on or inside the body. Their objects are outside *(bāhiresu)*: for the eyes, a vision, color, shape, or light; for the ears, sound; for the nose, smell; for the tongue, taste; for the body, something tangible; for the mind, a thought, emotion, fantasy or dream. Although called external, they become objects only when in contact with the internal *āyatanas,* on the framework of the body. For someone blind from birth there is no world of color, light, shape or form and no way of understanding that world. Six internal *āyatanas* and six external *āyatanas,* make twelve in all, and the *bāhiresu āyatana* only actually exist for us when each is in contact with its respective sense door.

How is the work done with the six internal and external sense spheres?

> *cakkhuṃ ca pajānāti, rūpe ca pajānāti, yaṃ ca tadubhayaṃ paṭicca uppajjati saṃyojanaṃ taṃ ca pajānāti...*

The truth of *cakkhu* (the eye sense door) and its object, *rūpa* (the shape or form) is realized: *pajānāti. Yaṃ ca tadubhayaṃ paṭicca,* with the base of these two, because of their contact, *uppajjati saṃyojanaṃ*—a bondage arises.

> *...yathā ca anuppannassa saṃyojanassa uppādo hoti taṃ ca pajānāti...*

The meditator works with this bondage that has now arisen: *saṃyojanassa uppādo hoti taṃ ca pajānāti.* The reality is that with every contact there is vibration, *phassa-paccayā vedanā. Saññā* evaluates: female, male; beautiful, ugly; pleasant, unpleasant. With this evaluation the sensations become pleasant or unpleasant, and immediately *saṅkhāra,* the reacting part of the mind, starts generating craving or aversion. Thus this whole process of bondage starts and multiplies.

The work with the six sense doors is within the boundary of mind and matter. It is a matter of analyzing and continually understanding how everything happens. If you are ignorant you constantly tie new knots and multiply bondage after bondage. When you don't react, as you experience and observe the bondage in wisdom, it weakens. The habit pattern of reaction starts changing. The old bondages can come on the surface: *yathā ca anuppannassa saṃyojanassa uppādo hoti tañ ca pajānāti.* You observe the arising *(uppāda)* of the bondage which had not previously come up *(anuppanna).*

> *...yathā ca uppannassa saṃyojanassa pahānaṃ hoti taṃ ca pajānāti, yathā ca pahīnassa saṃyojanassa āyatiṃ anuppādo hoti taṃ ca pajānāti.*

As you observe, the bondages get eradicated *(pahānaṃ)* one after the other: *yathā ca uppannassa samyojannassa pahānaṃ hoti tañ ca pajānāti.* When they have all come to the surface and passed away they do not again arise *(āyatiṃ anuppādo).* The stage beyond bondage, of total liberation, is reached.

There are three types of eradication. Even when you just observe *sīla,* because at the surface level of the mind you are not overreacting with craving or aversion, there is momentary eradication of your bondage. When you go deeper with *samādhi,* there is more eradication: the roots are shaken. Then when you practice Vipassana these roots are eradicated at the deepest level of the mind—*pahānaṃ.* For example, a thirsty person comes to drink at a pond with a surface covered by poisonous weeds. The weeds are pushed aside by hand from a small area, for temporary access; but afterwards they again cover this small area. This is momentary eradication. This is *sīla.* For better access, four poles with nets between are set up to hold back the weeds. This is *samādhi* which, as it goes deeper, clears a larger area, but leaves the roots. *Paññā* removes all the weeds, so that not a particle remains. This is real *pahāna* at the root level, which is what is meant here: *yathā ca pahīnassa saṃyojanassa āyatiṃ anuppādo hoti taṃ ca pajānāti.* Total eradication of the bondages is realized; they cannot again arise *(anuppādo).* This is the stage of the *arahant,* of total liberation.

> *Sotaṃ ca pajānāti, sadde ca pajānāti, yaṃ ca tadubhayaṃ paṭicca uppajjati saṃyojanaṃ taṃ ca pajānāti...*

Similarly the ear, the sound, and the bondage that arises because of them is observed.

> *...yathā ca anuppannassa saṃyojanassa uppādo hoti taṃ ca pajānāti, yathā ca uppannassa saṃyojanassa pahānaṃ hoti taṃ ca pajānāti, yathā ca pahīnassa saṃyojanassa āyatiṃ anuppādo hoti taṃ ca pajānāti.*

As equanimity develops, such bondages which had never previously come to the surface do so and are eradicated. This also is observed.

> *Ghānaṃ ca pajānāti, gandhe ca pajānāti...*
> *Jivhaṃ ca pajānāti, rase ca pajānāti...*
> *Kāyaṃ ca pajānāti, phoṭṭhabbe ca pajānāti...*
> *Manaṃ ca pajānāti, dhamme ca pajānāti...āyatiṃ anuppādo hoti taṃ ca pajānāti.*

Similarly the reality of nose and smell, tongue and taste, body and anything tangible, and mind and contents *(dhamme)* are observed *(pajānāti).* In each case the bondages arise, are eradicated, and do not come again. In each case the stage of an *arahant* is not merely accepted philosophically, but is experienced, witnessed: *pajānāti.*

> *Iti ajjhattaṃ vā dhammesu dhammānupassī viharati...'atthi dhamma' ti...na ca kiñci loke upādiyati.*

The same process follows. "This is *dhamma.*" All the six sense doors and their objects are mere *dhammas,* with no "I," "mine," "he," or "she," no individual there. Dividing, dissecting, disintegrating and dissolving, analyzing each sense door separately, the individual becomes just a mass, a process, an interaction of all of the *āyatanas* combined. With mere intellectual understanding, ignorance will prevent the witnessing of this *dhamma,* this process, and the escape from this bondage.

The practice leads through the same stations to the final goal.

Bojjhaṅgapabbaṃ— The Factors of Enlightenment

dhammesu dhammānupassī viharati sattasu bojjhaṅgesu

The *bojjhaṅgas* are the seven factors of enlightenment or qualities to be developed to reach the final goal.

The mind by itself is very pure: *viññāṇa* is very pure, but because of past *saṅkhāras,* conditioned *saññā* always gives a wrong evaluation, and when the sensation arises, *saṅkhāra* after *saṅkhāra* is again created. Because of this entire process the mind loses its own nature of purity and becomes very agitated. *Bojjhaṅgas* restore this purity: as they are observed as a reality, they increase to become perfect and when each is perfect, enlightenment is perfect. This is the whole process of Vipassana.

The first *bojjhaṅga* is *sati,* awareness. Without it, further steps on the path cannot be taken. *Sati,* objective observation of reality, is the most important factor because it must be continuously present from moment to moment with every other factor.

Dhamma-vicaya is second. The word *caya* or *cayana* means "to integrate." Apparent, consolidated, integrated, illusionary truth creates so much delusion and confusion: every decision and action goes wrong. *Vicaya* or *vicayana* means to divide, dissect, disintegrate, separate, as Vipassana intends you to do. Initially *dhamma-vicaya* is intellectual. The body is analyzed as just four elements, with no "I" about it. The mind is just the four aggregates. The six sense doors, their respective objects, the contact and process of multiplication are observed. The intellectual clarity gained gives guidance to start the actual practice of Vipassana and study the truth at the actual level.

The third *bojjhaṅga* is *viriya* (effort) as in *sammā-vāyāmo* in the Noble Eightfold Path. Great effort is required, but the effort is not to react, to let things just happen. Even if you have been victorious in a thousand battles against a thousand warriors, this inner battle of nonreaction is more difficult because the old habit is to do something, to react. Don't fight Ānanda's battle—"I *must* become an arahant," "I *must*" eradicate my impurities—if you do, the mind becomes unbalanced. Another extreme is not to work, not to observe at all, and just let things happen. Let things happen, but also know the reality as it is. Some slight degree of tension is necessary: either too much, or none at all, doesn't work. For example some pressure is necessary to drill a hole in a precious gem, but too much will break it. It is a middle path.

Viriya is to just observe, understanding the impermanent nature of arising and passing: practicing without reaction. The liberation is done by Dhamma, by the law of nature.

As you keep practicing with *sati, dhamma-vicaya,* and *viriya,* the impurities go away, and *pīti* comes and grows: pleasant sensation in the body, rapture, and bliss. You have to be careful. If you develop attachment to this free flow of subtle vibrations throughout the body, if you look for it and cling to it, it is no longer a *bojjhaṅga.* If the understanding of *anicca* remains—that this is still the field of mind and matter, of arising and passing—then the impurity goes away, and *pīti* develops and becomes a factor of enlightenment.

As wave after wave of this pleasant sensation comes and is observed, the important stage of *passaddhi* comes: deep tranquillity and calmness. Now even a slight sound is a great disturbance. Even the breath which becomes like a fine thread, making a subtle U-turn at the entrance of the nostrils, is a disturbance. The mind is so peaceful, quiet, tranquil. Again a danger comes: the false impression that this deep peace, never experienced before, is liberation. Just as *pīti,* the bliss, may become a bondage if not used properly, in the same way this *passaddhi* also may become a bondage. It is only a midway resthouse: the final goal is still far away. You can check that the six sense doors are still functioning: open your eyes, or listen. You are still in the field of arising and passing. You have not transcended the field of mind and matter.

Although difficult to grasp at this high stage, a subtle oscillation remains, and this sensation is called *adukkham-asukhaṃ.* In *pīti* it was pleasant; now it is just peaceful, and the danger is that *anicca* is not experienced. Detachment from craving towards pleasant sensation or aversion towards unpleasant sensation is much easier than detachment from this feeling of peace. Be very attentive: with a very sharp mind, feel the subtle oscillation, check the six sense doors, and keep understanding that this experience is *anicca.*

There is often a question about neutral sensation. The Buddha did not mean the initial, surface sensation which is neither pleasant nor unpleasant. That is totally different. It involves craving and aversion because people get bored with it, lose interest, and want something else. Their experience has become stale. They want something more or new, something they don't have. This is their old habit pattern.

Different people from different sects, communities, countries, religions, beliefs, and dogmas come to this Ganges of Vipassana to quench their thirst, to end ignorance and misery. Even when the mind-matter structure is accepted as arising and passing, and essenceless, because of their background this deep, neutral sensation gives an illusion of eternity, and so can become a bondage. To someone with a traditional belief in eternal soul, *passaddhi* seems to be this. To another with a belief in an eternal creator living inside us, it seems to be the unchanging creator. This is a dangerous illusion. Thoroughly examine this *passaddhi,* this deep, tranquil, calm experience. If you are aware of the very subtle oscillation, arising and passing, then it becomes a *bojjhaṅga* and gives you the strength to move further. Your experience grows.

The next enlightenment factor is *samādhi*—concentration or absorption. There were different types of *samādhis* before the Buddha became Buddha, as there are today. When eight *jhānas* are attained, there is a danger of feeling that the goal is attained, but this is only *lokiya samādhi,* which life after life results in rotation from one plane of existence to another. *Sammā-samādhi* takes us out of all the planes and gives full liberation from the bondage of birth and death, and from every type of suffering. It is practiced with *sampajañña,* the awareness of the mind-matter phenomenon and the realization of its nature of arising and passing. The mind is concentrated on reality. Then it becomes *lokuttara,* beyond the planes. As the *jhāna* is attained, simultaneously the fruit of *nibbāna* is attained. With *samādhi,* one after the other, the meditator attains the fruit of *sotāpanna, sakadāgāmī, anāgāmī,* and *arahant.* Then *samādhi* becomes an enlightenment factor.

Upekkhā—equanimity is the seventh factor of enlightenment. Like *sati,* it must be present from the beginning to the end, at every step. Whatever other factor is worked on, awareness and equanimity must always be there.

A pure mind has all these factors. Impurities, as they are observed, come to the surface and get eradicated; but these enlightenment factors, as they are observed, one by one, come on the surface, develop, multiply and become totally fulfilled. This section explains how the final goal of full enlightenment is thus reached.

santaṃ vā ajjhattaṃ satisambojjhaṅgaṃ 'atthi me ajjhattaṃ satisambojjhaṅgo' ti pajānāti, asantaṃ vā ajjhattaṃ

> *satisambojjhaṅgaṃ 'natthi me ajjhattaṃ satisambojjhaṅgo' ti pajānāti*

When the enlightenment factor of *sati* is present *(santaṃ)* the meditator understands *(pajānāti)—Atthi me ajjhattaṃ...'* ("Now it is present in me.") When it is *asantaṃ* (not present) the meditator accepts this reality also—*'N'atthi me ajjhattaṃ...'* ("Now it is not present in me.")

> *...yathā ca anuppannassa satisambojjhaṅgassa uppādo hoti taṃ ca pajānāti, yathā ca uppannassa satisambojjhaṅgassa bhāvanāya pāripūrī hoti taṃ ca pajānāti.*

All the past accumulated enlightenment factors of *sati* now help. They now come on the surface *(anuppannassa uppādo hoti)* and the meditator understands *(taṃ ca pajānāti)*. Having repeatedly arisen *(uppannassa)* they are understood with wisdom and multiply till they become complete—totally and fully attained *(bhāvanāya pāripūrī)*.

> *Santaṃ vā ajjhattaṃ dhammavicayasambojjhaṅgaṃ... bhāvanāya pāripūrī hoti taṃ ca pajānāti.*

Similarly *dhamma-vicaya,* analytical study of the truth, is understood as simply being present or absent. The past *dhamma-vicaya,* which had not arisen earlier, repeatedly arises from the depth of the mind and is observed: it develops to fulfillment and the final goal is reached. All this is understood.

> *...vīriyasambojjhaṅgaṃ...*
> *...pītisambojjhaṅgaṃ...*
> *...passaddhisambojjhaṅgaṃ...*
> *...samādhisambojjhaṅgaṃ...*
> *Santaṃ vā ajjhattaṃ upekkhāsambojjhaṅgaṃ... bhāvanāya pāripūrī hoti taṃ ca pajānāti.*

The enlightenment factors of *viriya* (effort), *pīti* (rapture, bliss, while feeling pleasant sensation in the body), *passaddhi* (tranquillity), *samādhi* (concentration) and *upekkhā* (equanimity) are understood in the same way and develop to completion.

> *Iti ajjhattaṃ vā dhammesu dhammānupassī viharati... 'atthi dhamma' ti...na ca kiñci loke upādiyati.*

Dhammas are observed inside, outside, and both inside and outside; arising, passing, and both arising and passing. The meditator realizes, "These are *dhammas*" and the awareness gets established with this reality. There is no more grasping or clinging. Thus *dhammānupassanā* is practiced.

✧

Questions And Answers

Q: Is directing our attention the only freedom we have, all other things being governed by Dhamma?

A: Everything is governed by Dhamma. Directing your attention is the only way to liberate yourself. You can do anything you wish, but if you react, Dhamma will bind you. If you just observe, Dhamma will certainly liberate you. This is the law of nature.

Q: Where is the dividing line between seriousness of practice and craving?

A: This is a good question. If you crave to work seriously, you are craving attainment of the result, or at least developing an attachment to working seriously. If you find yourself not working seriously and you then become depressed, there was craving. Just accept the fact that you were not working seriously and start again, knowing that you must work seriously. Then you keep progressing.

Q: Do neutral sensations come from neutral reactions, and do we hope to change this to mere observation?

A: Neutral sensations come because of ignorance. The ignorance goes when they are just observed as a changing phenomenon. A surface understanding of *anicca,* which is helpful, comes when after some time a very gross, solidified, unpleasant sensation goes. A deeper understanding, based on awareness of the subtle undercurrent of vibration, is that this sensation arises and passes every moment.

Q: When a meditator is carried away and rolls in thoughts of sense desire for some time before observation, is he multiplying the *saṅkhāras* to a worse state rather than purifying?

A: Previously the process of multiplication was continuous. Now your few moments of observation will turn into a few seconds, a few minutes, a few hours, which go to your credit. Practicing Vipassana, you understand that every time you roll in sense desires, you multiply your misery, and as much as you observe you are coming out of it.

Q: The Buddha's teaching seems to imply a sweeping movement of the attention related to the breath. What then is the origin and importance of working part by part in this practice?

A: When the Buddha says *sabba-kāya-paṭisaṃvedī assasissāmī' ti sikkhati, "sikkhati"* means "learns." Elsewhere *pajānāti* ("he understands properly") is used. You have to learn to sweep the whole body with one breath, and this learning is—observing part by part, allowing its solidity to dissolve, until the whole body is dissolved and you can sweep the entire mass. Then again you go part by part because even though the whole body seems opened up, there might be small unknown areas. You learn *(sikkhati)* to reach the stage of *bhaṅga-ñāṇa.*

Q: The *Sutta* outlines four observations and numerous practices, yet you teach only respiration and sensation on the body. There is no ranking of practices by order of importance. Why not also teach all practices such as walking meditation and noting ideas?

A: There are different traditions, and the Buddha, an enlightened person, also gave different initial objects to different people according to their background, capacity and inclination. However, as they proceeded, the stations were the same.

This living tradition comes from the initial practice of respiration, from which the meditator goes on to experience sensation, and thus arising and passing. Awareness of respiration and sensation together will lead to the final goal. It is not prohibited to try something else, but if you are progressing here, trying elsewhere just out of curiosity will waste your time. If you already feel sensation everywhere and now somewhere else you try observing walking—each foot moving up and down, but without sensation—your faculty of feeling sensation at a subtle level will get blunted. Reverting again to this technique you won't be able to feel sensations at that depth. Of course there are people with very gross, rough types of mind for whom subtle respiration is very difficult, and walking may suit them better.

It is also difficult to feel subtle breath in a small area. If you are already feeling it clearly and then you try to feel it with your hand on the stomach—which is such a crude technique—you are regressing. The Buddha intends you to move from *olāriko* to *sukhuma*—from the gross to the subtle. If at a certain stage something gross arises from the depths, it can't be helped; but just out of curiosity you cannot afford to start intentionally working with a gross object, such as the first sentences of another technique, forgetting all about the subtle reality of the station you had already reached. If another technique suits you better, stick to it and reach the final goal: but time is essential. Don't waste your precious life running here and there.

Q: "I" is not.

A: Yes—"I" is not!

Q: What is it then that needs enlightening?

A: Ignorance needs enlightening, bondage needs liberation. Nothing else.

Q: How do you define a mind of compassion? Can we use compassion with awareness when dealing with our own suffering?

A: When compassion is in your mind, accept your mind as a mind of compassion. Certainly be kind to yourself, love yourself, be the first object of your own compassion. Every time you generate *saṅkhāras,* even craving and aversion towards someone else, you cruelly inflict so much misery on yourself. Your anger will not harm a good Vipassana meditator—it may or may not harm others—but you yourself are harmed and become miserable. Avoid it. Be kind and compassionate to yourself.

Q: Is it true that the interpretation of *vedanā* most distinguishes our form of Vipassana from others in the Buddhist tradition? And how do the others define *vedanā,* if not as physical sensations?

A: Yes. Other traditions take *vedanā* only as feelings of the mind. We don't condemn others and it is true that *vedanā* is one of the four aggregates of the mind. We have to explain rather than just translate because some words used by the Buddha had already been explained previously by him. For instance, *sampajañña* had been explained as the feeling of sensations arising and passing. Also, many words today are either lost or carry totally different meanings, so that we have to go to the *Tipiṭaka* to find the Buddha's original definition of them. The Buddha had explained that *sukha* and *dukkha vedanā* referred to the body, and he used *somanassa* and *domanassa* to refer to the mind. In *vedanānupassanā* he doesn't use *somanassa* and *domanassa,* but *sukha* and *dukkha vedanā,* so we have to work with sensations on the body.

✧

Whatever you have understood intellectually and whatever you have experienced, make use of it. Make use of Dhamma not only on this course but in daily life. Reaction is always full of negativity. Live the life of Dhamma. Whatever happens outside, observe the reality of sensations inside and remain equanimous, then all your decisions and all your actions will be healthy—not reactions, but positive actions, good for you and good for others.

May all of you be able to lead a life good for both yourself and others. May you all enjoy the best fruits of Dhamma: peace, harmony, happiness.

May all beings be happy.

DAY SEVEN

THE SEVENTH DAY of the *Satipaṭṭhāna* course is over. We reach the closing part of the *Mahā-satipaṭṭhāna Sutta.*

Catusaccapabbaṃ—The Four Noble Truths

dhammesu dhammānupassī viharati catūsu ariyasaccesu

How is *dhammānupassanā* practiced observing the Four Noble Truths?

'idaṃ dukkhaṃ' ti yathābhūtaṃ pajānāti, 'ayaṃ dukkha-samudayo' ti yathābhūtaṃ pajānāti, 'ayaṃ dukkhanirodho' ti yathābhūtaṃ pajānāti, 'ayaṃ dukkhanirodhagāminī paṭipadā' ti yathābhūtaṃ pajānāti.

"This is suffering." "This is the arising of suffering." "This is the total cessation of suffering." "This is the path which leads to the total cessation of suffering." Each truth is understood as it is.

Pajānāti means to understand in wisdom. *Yathābutaṃ*—as it is, as it happens—means direct experience and understanding, as taught in the Buddha's first discourse. The fact that suffering resulted from craving was already known. That craving had to be eradicated was not new. Everyone is suffering, but that fact by itself does not make anyone a noble person. The Buddha's discovery was how to make it an *ariya sacca,* a noble truth, so that whoever experiences it becomes a noble person, attains at least the first experience of *nibbāna,* the first stage of liberation.

For each of the Four Noble Truths three things are necessary, making twelve in all. The first part of the First Noble

Truth—"This is suffering"—is understood by everybody. The second part, *pariññeyya,* means however that every aspect of suffering must be understood, the entire field. The same word *parijānāti* was previously used for the total understanding of *vedanā,* with *sampajañña. Parijānāti* comes when *vedanā* is transcended. If not, some part of the field of *vedanā* might still be unexplored. Similarly the entire field of *dukkha* has to be explored, up to its limit. Then the third part comes: *pariññāta,* "It is totally explored." This means that it is transcended: it is an *ariya sacca.* The claim to have explored the entire field of *dukkha* can only be made when it is transcended.

On the surface there are four Noble Truths, but as you go deeper they culminate in one, like the four *satipaṭṭhānas.*

Dukkha samudaya, the arising or cause of suffering—that is, craving—is the Second Noble Truth. Again, intellectual acceptance and surface understanding of this basic principle survive from the teachings of previous Buddhas. However the second part of it is *pahātabbaṃ:* craving should be totally eradicated. Then comes the third, *pahīnaṃ:* it is totally eradicated; the stage of final liberation is reached. The Buddha's contribution was to reestablish this deeper aspect, which had long ago disappeared.

Similarly mere acceptance of the Third Noble Truth—*dukkha nirodha,* the cessation of suffering—out of devotion or logic is insufficient. Its second part is *sacchikātabbaṃ:* it is to be witnessed. Its third stage is *sacchikataṃ:* it has been witnessed, and so is complete.

The Fourth Noble Truth of the Path is also meaningless if it is merely accepted intellectually. Its second part is *bhāvetabbaṃ:* it has to be practiced repeatedly until *bhāvitaṃ,* its full completion. Only when he had walked on the whole Path, only when he had completed all Four Noble Truths, each in these three ways, did Gotama call himself a Buddha.

Initially the five friends to whom he first gave Dhamma would not even listen to the Buddha. They believed that liberation was impossible without practicing extreme bodily torture. The Buddha had already practiced this. He had starved his body until it was a mere skeleton, too weak to take even two steps. Yet with his earlier practice of eight *jhānas,* he had seen that the deeper impurities still remained. Starving the body was a futile exercise, so he had given it up and started eating.

To convince them he told them that he had witnessed the Four Noble Truths *yathābhūtaṃ pajānāti:* with experiential wisdom as they happen, not just intellectually or devotionally. Only then were they prepared at least to start listening to him.

Dukkhasaccaṃ—The Truth of Suffering

dukkhaṃ ariyasaccaṃ

The Noble Truth of Suffering is now described, from the gross to the subtle.

> *Jāti pi dukkhā, jarā pi dukkhā, (byādhi pi dukkhā,) maraṇaṃ pi dukkhaṃ, sokaparidevadukkhadomanassupāyāsā pi dukkhā, appiyehi sampayogo pi dukkho, piyehi vippayogo pi dukkho, yampicchaṃ na labhati taṃ pi dukkhaṃ, saṅkhittena pañcupādānakkhandhā dukkhā.*

Each manifestation of *dukkha* is explained using synonyms.

Jāti is birth in whatever plane of existence. *Jarā* is old age, frailty, the deterioration of the sense faculties. *Byādhi* is disease or sickness. *Maraṇa* is death from whatever plane of existence, and the dissolution of the aggregates. *Soka* is sorrow, mental grief from the loss of something very dear, and *parideva* is the crying and lamenting that results. *Dukkha* is bodily pain and unpleasant sensation. *Domanassa* is mental unpleasantness. *Upāyāsa* is mental distress and affliction following loss or misfortune. All these are *dukkha.*

Both here and in other explanations, *dukkha* is used for unpleasant or painful bodily sensation, and *domanassa* (from *mana,* mind) for mental unpleasantness. It could be a thought, a memory, a fear. Similarly *sukha* is used for pleasant bodily sensation and *somanassa* for pleasant feeling in the mind. In *vedanānupassanā* the words *dukkha* and *sukha vedanā* are used, which is why this tradition strongly emphasizes bodily sensations as the object of meditation.

At a subtler level *appiyehi sampayogo* is association with anything unpleasant: *rūpa,* a vision, color or light; *sadda,* sound; *gandha,* smell; *rasa,* taste; *phoṭṭabba,* touch; or *dhamma,* a thought. *Piyehi vippayogo* is disassociation from anything pleasant. Disassociation from those who are dear, such as friends and family members, is *dukkha*

Still subtler is *iccham̱ na labhati:* not getting what is desired. If someone desires to escape the cycle of birth, but does not reach this stage, it is *na pattabbaṃ,* not fulfilled. This is misery. Similarly desire arises to be free of old age, illness, death, and of all mental and physical grief and pain, and it is not fulfilled.

Saṅkhittena, in summary, and at a still deeper level, the*pañc-upādānakkhanda,* the *upādāna,* the attachment to the five aggregates, the*pañca khanda*—of *rūpa,* matter; *vedana,* sensation; *sañña,* perception; *saṅkhāra,* reaction; and *viññāṇa,* consciousness—is misery.

Devotional or logical acceptance of the First Noble Truth does not help: it has to be experienced *(yathābhūtaṃ pajānāti)* to its final limit. This is done by the practice of *sīla* and *samādhi,* and with a concentrated mind you practice the observation of the subtler reality of the workings of the five *khandhas* and the six sense doors. This is the whole process of the Noble Eightfold Path.

The initial solidified, intensified and painful sensations are obviously *dukkha,* but they have to be observed with equanimity because reaction to them will multiply the misery. By equanimity they are divided, dissected, disintegrated and dissolved, and even if pain remains, an undercurrent of vibrations is felt with it. When broken up by these wavelets it does not seem to be misery. When even this goes away, there is only a flow of very subtle vibrations, giving rise to *pīti.* This is still the field of *dukkha,* lacking any real happiness, because it is *anicca,* arising and passing. The first experience of *bhaṅga* is very important, just to realize the truth that the entire material structure is nothing but subatomic particles. If however it is regarded as freedom from misery, then the field of *dukkha* has not been fully covered. Unpleasant sensations will again come: partly because of the surfacing of deep past *saṇkhāras,* partly because of posture, illness, and the like. Every pleasant experience, because it is impermanent, has *dukkha* as its inherent nature.

The next stage, *passaddhi,* tranquillity, containing no unpleasantness and apparently no *dukkha,* still has *samudaya vaya* present. Yet *sabbe saṅkhārā aniccā*—whatever gets composed is sooner or later bound to be destroyed. Gross experiences will still come, because this *passaddhi* is still a passing experience, still in the field of mind and matter. The entire field of *dukkha* is not complete. It can be said to be explored only when it is transcended to a stage beyond, where nothing arises or is created.

Thus the understanding of *dukkha* at a gross level cannot be said to be a Noble Truth. *Parijānāti* (complete understanding) means exploring the entire field with direct experience. Only when it is *pariññātaṃ* (understood to its end) does it actually become a Noble Truth.

Samudayasaccaṃ—
The Truth of the Arising of Suffering

dukkhasamudayaṃ ariyasaccaṃ

The Second Noble Truth is the arising of misery.

Yāyaṃ taṇhā ponobbhavikā nandīrāgasahagatā tatratatrā-bhinandinī, seyyathidaṃ, kāmataṇhā bhavataṇhā vibhavataṇhā.

This is *taṇhā,* craving; *ponobbhavikā,* resulting in life after life; *nandī-rāga-sahagatā,* bound up with desire for pleasure; *tatra-tatrābhinandinī,* taking pleasure here and there; *seyyathīdaṃ,* that is:

Kāma-taṇhā is sensual pleasure. Any little desire so quickly turns into craving, and predominant is sexual desire.

Bhava-taṇhā is the desire to survive, even though the body and the entire universe are continually destroyed. Because of this ego, because of craving towards becoming, philosophies which espouse eternity seem attractive.

Vibhava-taṇhā is the opposite in two ways. One is desiring this circle of life and death to stop, a stage which cannot be attained by such unbalanced craving. A second is refusing to accept the continuation of misery after death, while there are still *saṅkhāras,* out of fear of the results of the unwholesome actions of this life. There is an unbalanced craving and clinging to the philosophy that: "This is the only existence."

These three *taṇhās* result in *dukkha.*

Where then does this *taṇhā* arise and stay?

Yaṃ loke piyarūpaṃ sātarūpaṃ etthesā taṇhā uppajjamānā uppajjati, ettha nivisamānā nivisati.

Craving *uppajjati* (arises) and *nivisati* (stays) wherever in the *loka* there is pleasure *(loke piyarūpaṃ sātarūpaṃ).* Both *pīya* and *sāta* mean "pleasant", "agreeable." One meaning of *loka* is "planes of existence," but here it means "within the framework of the body." A *deva* called Rohita once passed in front of the monastery where the Buddha was sitting, and this person was singing: *Caraiveti, caraiveti,* "Keep walking, keep walking." Questioned by the Buddha, Rohita said he was walking to explore the entire *loka* and then beyond. The

Buddha smiled, and explained that the entire universe, its cause, its cessation, and the way to its cessation are within the framework of the body.

Literally *luñjati paluñjatī ti loka*—the *loka* is continually being destroyed. It arises and passes away. It is the entire field of mind and matter, and it is understood within the framework of the body. As you plant the seed of a particular plane of existence, you experience it. A very unwholesome *saṅkhāra* will result in hellfire within, both now and later, when the fruit comes. Planting the seed of a heavenly plane, you feel pleasant; of a *brāhmic* plane, you feel tranquil, both now and later. The stage of *nibbāna* also, where nothing arises or passes, has to be experienced within the body.

Craving therefore arises wherever something pleasant is felt, within the framework of the body. Now details are given about where the craving arises.

> *Cakkhu loke piyarūpaṃ sātarūpaṃ, etthesā taṇhā uppajjamānā uppajjati, ettha nivisamānā nivisati... Sotaṃ... Ghānaṃ... Jivhā... Kāyo... Mano loke piyarūpaṃ sātarūpaṃ, etthesā taṇhā uppajjamānā uppajjati, ettha nivisamānā nivisati.*

Craving arises and stays at the *cakkhu*—the eye sense door—which is pleasant and agreeable. The same process occurs with ear, nose, tongue, body or mind.

> *Rūpa... Saddā... Gandhā... Rasā... Phoṭṭhabbā... Dhammā... nivisati.*

Wherever pleasure is felt in the object, such as a vision, sound, smell, taste, touch or thought, craving arises and stays.

> *Cakkhu-viññāṇaṃ... Sota-viññāṇaṃ... Ghāna-viññāṇaṃ... Jivhā-viññāṇaṃ... Kāya-viññāṇaṃ... Mano-viññāṇaṃ... nivisati.*

Craving arises at any of the six *viññāṇas* of the sense doors. As a description of mind, the four aggregates of *viññāṇa*, *saññā, vedanā,* and *saṅkhāra* generally suffice. Deeper Vipassana separates them. Before that stage is reached however, philosophies start because, despite the experience of arising and passing, the observer—which is *viññāṇa*—seems to remain and it is not divided or dissected. It is viewed as eternal soul: *je viññāya te āya ye āya te viññāya* (Whatever is *viññāṇa* is soul and whatever is soul is *viññāṇa*). However at a deeper level it does become separated: eye *viññāṇa* cannot hear, ear *viññāṇa* cannot see, any or all of these *viññāṇas* can stop, and when mind *viññāṇa* also stops, *nibbāna* comes.

The Buddha gives further details:

> *Cakkhu-samphasso...*
> *Cakkhu-samphassajā vedanā...*
> *Rūpa-saññā...*
> *Rūpa-sañcetanā...*
> *Rūpa-taṇhā...*
> *Rūpa-vitakko...*
> *Rūpa-vicāro... nivisati.*

Because of contact *(samphasso)* at any sense door craving also arises and stays. Because of this contact there is a sensation *(samphassajā vedana)* and again craving arises and stays. Then follows evaluation or perception *(saññā)* of the object of the sense door, and craving arises and stays. *Sañcetanā* (mental reaction) towards the object is a synonym of *saṅkhāra:* here again craving arises and stays. Then craving *(taṇhā)* arises and stays in relation to any of the sense objects. Initial application of thought to the object *(vitakko)* follows. Finally follows the rolling in the thought *(vicāro)*. In every case the entire process happens at each of the six sense doors.

This Second Noble Truth is called *dukkha-samudaya*. In general understanding it is true that *taṇhā* is the cause of suffering. However, *samudaya* means "arising," because suffering arises simultaneously with craving, with no time gap.

Nirodhasaccaṃ—
The Truth of the Cessation of Suffering

dukkhanirodhaṃ ariyasaccaṃ

The Third Noble Truth is the total eradication of craving so that it does not arise again at all. "It is the complete fading away and cessation of this very craving, forsaking it and giving it up; the liberation from it, leaving no place for it."

> *Yo tassāyeva taṇhāya asesavirāganirodho cāgo paṭinissaggo mutti anālayo.*

Where is this work done?

> *Yaṃ loke piyarūpaṃ sātarūpaṃ, etthesā taṇhā pahīyamānā pahīyati, ettha nirujjhamānā nirujjhati.*

Wherever *taṇhā* (craving) arises and stays in the *loke*—the field of mind and matter—there it is to be eradicated *(pahīyamānā pahīyati)* and extinguished *(nirujjhamānā nirujjhati)*. It must be worked on and totally eradicated at the eye, the ear, the nose, the tongue, the body, and the mind sense doors. Details are now again given:

> *Cakkhu... Sotaṃ... Ghānaṃ... Jivhā... Kāyo... Mano loke piyarūpaṃ sātarūpaṃ, etthesā taṇhā pahīyamānā pahīyati, ettha nirujjhamānā nirujjhati.*

> *Rūpa... Saddā... Gandhā... Rasā... Phoṭṭhabbā... Dhammā... nirujjhati.*

> *Cakkhu-viññāṇaṃ...*
> *Cakkhu-samphasso...*
> *Cakkhu-samphassajā vedanā...*
> *Rūpa-saññā...*
> *Rūpa-sañcetanā...*
> *Rūpa-taṇhā...*
> *Rūpa-vitakko...*
> *Rūpa-vicāro... nirujjhati.*

The cessation must be total, both in the six sense doors and their related objects. Again six *viññāṇas* precede both the contact and its resulting sensation. Then follow six *saññās*, which evaluates the sensation. Then there are six *sañcetanās* (volitional actions), that can also be called *saṅkhāras*. *Taṇhā* (craving) follows. *Vitakko* is the beginning of thought in reaction to the contact of object and sense door, or the beginning of remembering or thinking of the future, in relation to the contact. *Vitakka* is followed by *vicāro* which is continuous thinking, in relation to the object.

This is the Noble Truth of the Cessation of Suffering. In this course such minute, detailed analysis at the experiential level is totally impossible, but the *Sutta* is a complete teaching. Its audience would have included those working on the third or fourth stage of *nibbāna*, from *ānāgāmī* to *arahant*. At these high stages every detail is separated, and laid bare. You understand every little sensation that arises, how it relates to a particular sense door, and how to the object of the sense door. You understand now how it arises related to *saññā*, to *sancetanā*, and to the *saṅkhāra;* and you understand how it ceases, related to this or that. At such a very high stage, each can be divided and dissected in minute detail. Now, and even at the stage of *sotāpanna*, the reality, although deep, is not that deep; therefore understanding whether or not there is craving or aversion as a result of some sensation—together with the understanding of *anicca*—is enough.

Maggasaccaṃ—The Truth of the Path

dukkhanirodhagāminī paṭipadā ariyasaccaṃ

The Fourth Noble Truth is the Path for the eradication of suffering.

ariyo aṭṭhaṅgiko maggo, seyyathidaṃ, sammādiṭṭhi, sammāsaṅkappo, sammāvācā, sammākammanto, sammāājīvo, sammāvāyāmo, sammāsati, sammāsamādhi.

The Path is eightfold. Each part is now explained.

Right understanding *(sammādiṭṭhi)* is:

dukkhe ñāṇaṃ, dukkhasamudaye ñāṇaṃ, dukkhanirodhe ñāṇaṃ, dukkhanirodhagāminiyā paṭipadāya ñāṇaṃ.

It is total experiential wisdom about misery, its arising, its cessation, and the path: *yathā-bhūtaṃ pajānāti,* proper understanding of the reality as it is.

Right thoughts *(sammāsaṅkappo)* are:

nekkhammasaṅkappo, abyāpādasaṅkappo, avihiṃsāsaṅkappo.

They are thoughts of renunciation, thoughts which are free of anger, and thoughts which are free from violence.

Right speech *(sammāvācā)* is:

musāvādā veramaṇī, pisuṇāya vācāya veramaṇī, pharusāya vācāya veramaṇī, samphappalāpā veramaṇī.

It is not false or hurtful. It is not backbiting or slander. Again understand that this must be *yathā-bhūtaṃ pajānāti.* It must happen in your life. It must be experienced, along with the understanding that you are living a life of abstinence from false, hurtful, backbiting, or slanderous talk. Unless you are practicing this, unless it is experienced, unless it is happening in your life, it is not *sammā* but *micchā,* merely an intellectual or emotional game. It must be *yathābhūta.*

Right action *(sammākammanto)* is:

pāṇātipātā veramaṇī, adinnādānā veramaṇī, kāmesumicchācārā veramaṇī.

It is abstinence at the bodily level *(veramaṇī)* from killing *(pāṇātipātā)*, stealing *(adinnādānā)* or sexual misconduct *(kāmesumicchācārā)*. This must also be experienced; it must happen in life. Only when you can say that you are living a life of abstinence from killing, stealing and sexual misconduct is it *pajānāti*, is it experienced as it is.

Right livelihood *(sammā-ājīvo)* is:

ariyasāvako micchā-ājīvaṃ pahāya sammā-ājīvena jīvitaṃ kappeti.

It is where unwholesome *(micchā)* livelihood has been given up *(pahāya)*, and again the same applies: the earning of a livelihood by wholesome means must be experienced in life.

Right effort *(sammāvāyāmo)* is fourfold:

anuppannānaṃ pāpakānaṃ akusalānaṃ dhammānaṃ anuppādāya...
uppannānaṃ pāpakānaṃ akusalānaṃ dhammānaṃ pahānāya...
anuppannānaṃ kusalānaṃ dhammānaṃ uppādāya...
uppannānaṃ kusalānaṃ dhammānaṃ ṭhitiyā asammosāya bhiyyobhāvāya vepullāya bhāvanāya pāripūriyā...
...chandaṃ janeti vāyamati vīriyaṃ ārabhati cittaṃ paggaṇhāti padahati.

It is to restrain unwholesome impurities *(pāpakānaṃ akusalānaṃ dhammānaṃ)* which are *anuppannānaṃ* (unarisen). It is to remove *uppannānaṃ* (arisen) impurity. It is to awaken wholesomeness *(kusalānaṃ dhammānaṃ)* which has not arisen. It is to retain, not to let fade, and to multiply arisen wholesomeness, up to its total fulfillment *(bhāvanāya pāripūriyā)*.

In each case the meditator "makes strong effort *(chandaṃ janeti vāyamati)*, stirs up his energy *(viriyaṃ ārabheti)*, applies his mind *(cittaṃ paggaṇhāti)* and strives *(padahati)*."

Right awareness *(sammāsati)* is:

kaye kāyānupassī viharati... vedanāsu vedanānupassī viharati... citte cittānupassī viharati... dhammesu dhammānupassī viharati ātāpī sampajāno satimā, vineyya loke abhijjhādomanassaṃ.

Wherever the Buddha describes *sati,* the description of the four fields of *satipaṭṭhāna* is repeated: that is, *sampajañña,* the experience of sensation arising and passing, must be present. Otherwise what is being practiced is not *sammā-sati,* but rather the ordinary awareness of a circus performer.

Right concentration *(sammāsamādhi)* is the practice of four *jhānas:*

vivicceva kāmehi vivicca akusalehi dhammehi savitakkaṃ savicāraṃ vivekajaṃ pītisukhaṃ...

vitakkavicārānaṃ vūpasamā ajjhattaṃ sampasādanaṃ cetaso ekodibhāvaṃ avitakkaṃ avicāraṃ samādhijaṃ pītisukhaṃ...

pītiyā ca virāgā upekkhako ca viharati sato ca sampajāno sukhaṃ ca kāyena paṭisaṃvedeti yaṃ taṃ ariyā ācikkhanti: 'upekkhako satimā sukhavihārī' ti...

sukhassa ca pahānā dukkhassa ca pahānā pubbeva somanassadomanassānaṃ atthaṅgamā adukkhamasukhaṃ upekkhāsatipārisuddhiṃ...

In the first *jhāna* there is detachment from sense desires *(kāmehi)* and mental impurities. It is *savitakkaṃ savicāraṃ*: with attention to the object of meditation and with continual awareness of the object. There is detachment *(vivekajaṃ)* and *pītisukhaṃ*—a lot of mental pleasantness with pleasant sensation on the body. The mind is concentrated. In the second *jhāna, vitakka-vicārānaṃ vūpasamā:* the meditation object recedes, and there is pleasantness in the mind and body. In the third *jhāna*, mental pleasantness (*pīti*) recedes: there is only *sukha*, a pleasant bodily sensation from mental concentration. However *sampajāna,* the reality of arising and passing away, is now added.

Understand that even before the Buddha became Buddha, the *jhānas* were present in India. He had learnt the seventh and eighth *jhānas* from two of his previous teachers. Yet here only four *jhānas* are taught. The reason is that in the *jhānas* which he had learnt previously, *sampajañña* was missing. As result, they could remove only the surface and slightly deeper impurities. Without *sampajañña*, they could not go to the depth and take out the deep-rooted impurities of the mind. These impurities remained, because of which the life continuum continued. Now with the practice of only four *jhānas*, in the third arising and passing are observed. *Sampajañña* is present.

In the fourth *jhāna*, there is no more *sukha* or *dukkha*. *Somanassa*, and *domanassa* are gone. There is neither pleasant nor unpleasant feeling in the mind. Only *adukkham-asukhaṃ* (tranquillity) remains, with *upekkha-sati-pārisuddhiṃ* (equanimity, awareness and total purification). *Sampajāno* is not now used because this is the *nibbānic* stage. The fourth *jhāna* comes together with the fourth *nibbānic* stage of the *arahant*. *Sampajañña* was the Buddha's contribution to the meditation practices of those days, the means with which to go beyond the entire field of mind and matter.

This is the Fourth Noble Truth.

> *Iti ajjhattaṃ vā dhammesu dhammānupassī viharati... 'atthi dhamma' ti...na ca kiñci loke upādiyati.*

The same stations recur: awareness is established in the truth of nothing but *dhamma* and then there is nothing to cling to.

This entire explanation has to be experienced and understood. We can read it, but only with deeper experience does the meaning of the Buddha's words become clear. At the stage of the *arahant* everything is clear by experience.

Satipaṭṭhānabhāvanānisaṃso—Results of the Practice

Practicing in this manner, one of two fruits is attained:

diṭṭheva dhamme aññā, sati vā upādisese anāgāmitā.

Either *diṭṭheva dhamme aññā*—the total understanding of an *arahant*—is attained, or the third stage of *anāgāmī* and that within seven years.

Someone who has been practicing more than seven years asks why they are not an *arahant.* The necessary condition however is *evaṃ bhāveya,* having practiced exactly as set out. It is *sampajaññaṃ na riñcati,* where *sampajañña* is not missed for any moment in life. Now you are preparing for this stage, practicing feeling sensation in everything you do at the physical level, and understanding arising and passing. When you can practice in this way you have the Buddha's guarantee of the results.

Further the Buddha says, leave aside seven years, six years, five, four, and even down to one year; then seven months, six, and down to one, even half a month, or even seven days will suffice. It differs depending on the past accumulation, even if *sampajañña* is practiced every moment. It might be seven years, yet practicing the same technique there were instances where someone experienced *nibbāna* after just a few minutes, like the person who came from Bombay and was taught only the words *diṭṭhe diṭṭhamattaṃ bhavissati.*

Some meditators start with walking, even mentally repeating "walking", "itching", or whatever. There is no *paññā*: but at least the practice concentrates the mind. Those with a strong sex desire, go to a cemetery—or nowadays an autopsy—to balance their minds somewhat. Whatever the starting point, the meditator must experience sensations as arising and passing. At this point your *sampajañña* may be only for a few seconds, and then forgotten for minutes or even hours together. With continual work, later you will forget *sampajañña* only briefly, then not even for a moment. That stage may take a long time, but after that the limit is seven years.

Then come the closing words:

'Ekāyano ayaṃ, bhikkhave, maggo sattānaṃ visuddhiyā, sokaparidevānaṃ samatikkamāya, dukkhadomanassānaṃ atthaṅgamāya, ñāyassa adhigamāya, nibbānassa sacchikiriyāya yadidaṃ cattāro satipaṭṭhānā' ti. Iti yaṃ taṃ vuttaṃ, idametaṃ paṭicca vuttaṃ ti.

"It is for this reason that it was said: 'This is the one and only way, monks, for the purification of beings, for the overcoming of sorrow and lamentation, for the extinguishing of suffering and grief, for walking on the path of truth, for the realization of *nibbāna:* that is to say, the fourfold establishing of awareness.'"

Ekāyano maggo is not a sectarian claim, but a law of nature. The path helps not only those who call themselves Buddhists or have implicit faith: it is to be experienced by one and all, practicing with and so transcending sensation. Whether or not there is a Buddha, universal law exists. The earth is round; gravity does exist; the law of relativity exists whether or not Galileo, Newton or Einstein discovers it. Similarly the arising and eradication of misery is a law. Just as two parts of hydrogen and one part of oxygen make water: so, when in deep ignorance there is a reaction of craving or aversion, misery arises. This is not Hindu, Buddhist or Christian law, but simply the law. Similarly if there is full awareness and *sampajañña,* understanding of the entire truth, there is liberation. Intellectual understanding can only give inspiration and guidance. Without even this, those of different views cannot explore and experience the truth. Someone might assert that the earth is flat, or that gravity does not exist, but nothing will change for them.

Fire will burn your hand. This truth can be experienced. To avoid it, keep your hand away from fire. In exactly the same way, reacting to sensations causes misery. If you stop reacting and just observe their arising and passing, naturally your practice will extinguish misery, the fire of craving and aversion, just as water extinguishes fire. This is *ekāyano maggo*—the law, truth, or nature for one and all.

Questions and Answers

Every word of the *Sutta* will become clear as you practice and reach the final goal. At this stage, many questions keep coming. Even if the Teacher's answers satisfy you intellectually, doubt may wash them away. You are only imagining, not seeing. Practice. In every course, as you keep experiencing Dhamma, you hear the same discourses, the same words, but you find something new each time. Real understanding, clear and free from any doubt or skepticism, comes with your own experience.

✧

Q. You mentioned noting various mental states arising. How should you deal with, say, anger or fantasy?

A. Noting anger, fear, passion, ego or any kind of impurity does not mean mentally reciting them. Noting may help you concentrate and understand somewhat, but *sampajañña* is missing. Just accept the mental content, that your mind is with, say, anger—*sadosaṃ vā cittaṃ pajānāti*—and observe any predominant sensation, with the understanding of arising and passing. Any sensation at that time will be connected to the anger.

Q. From where do *kalāpas* arise and to what do they pass away? Something cannot come from nothing.

A. Whence did the universe start, and how was it created? This is speculation, how all philosophies start. The Buddha called them all irrelevant questions. They have nothing to do with misery, its arising, its eradication, and the way to its eradication. Creation is going on every moment: *kalāpas* are created, they arise and pass, and ignorance of this arising and passing results in misery. Anything else is meaningless. Human life is short and you have such a big job to change the habit pattern of the mind at the deepest level and reach full liberation. Don't waste your time: work, and the reality of your experience will later on reveal everything.

Q. What is the cause behind the existence of this world of mind and matter?

A. Ignorance generates *saṅkhāras,* and *saṅkhāras* multiply ignorance. The entire universe is created by this mutual support, nothing else.

Q. How did ignorance begin? It could not coexist with love, wisdom, and knowledge.

A. Certainly, but it is more important to see the ignorance of this moment and let purity come. Otherwise it becomes a philosophical question, which doesn't help.

Q. Did the Buddha teach outside India, in Burma?

A. There is no evidence that he taught outside the Ganga-Jamuna area of northern India.

Q. With respect, how can we say that the Buddha rediscovered the lost technique when he was taught it and took his vow in front of a previous Buddha?

A. Many who meet a Buddha become inspired and desire not just to liberate themselves, but also to become a *Sammā-sambuddha* and help liberate many others. Expressing this desire, their mental capacity can be examined by the then *Sammā-sambuddha:* whether having already worked countless aeons they would, if now given Vipassana, very soon become *arahants:* and whether even though knowing this they still wish to develop their *pāramīs* to the necessary extent over countless further aeons. If so, they receive not just a blessing but a time prediction. The ascetic who later was born as Gotama, was capable of reaching the stage of an *arahant* then, but did not take Vipassana.

In his last life, with darkness all around, words highly praising Vipassana still existed in the ancient *Ṛg-Veda,* but were mere recitations. The practice was lost. Due to his past *pāramīs* he went to the depth and discovered it. He said *pubbe ananussutesu dhammesu cakkhuṃ udapādi:* "My eye is opened in a *dhamma* which I had never heard before." Later he called it *purāṇo maggo,* an ancient path. He rediscovered and distributed a dormant, forgotten path.

Q. Does an entity with *saṅkhāras* causing rebirth have any choice in the circumstances, or is it actually determined by past *saṅkhāras?*

A. The past *saṅkhāras* which are responsible for life in the lower fields are so powerful that at the time of death one of these will arise and generate a vibration which is in tune with the vibration of a particular plane; in that way you are sucked to deeper levels of misery. If however Vipassana has been properly practiced, even with such *saṅkhāras* the Vipassana vibration is so strong that at the last mind moment this arises and connects with a plane where Vipassana can be practiced, instead of a lower field. So in another way you can choose not to go down.

Q. If the "I" is nonexistent, an illusion, how can "I" be reincarnated?

A. Nothing is incarnated. There is a continuous flow of mind and matter: every moment *saṅkhāra-paccayā viññāṇaṃ.* At death the push of some deep *saṅkhāra* causes *viññāṇa* to arise with some other body.

Q. If the reward for achieving *nibbāna* is bodily death, why practice to die?

A. It is not annihilation, but a wonderful art of dying. It is also an art of living, coming out of impurities to lead a healthy life. When you experience *nibbāna,* it is something like death: the sense doors do not work, but you are fully awakened inside. Experience it. The question will be answered automatically.

Q. Where does a liberated person live without rebirth?

A. Many such questions were asked of the Buddha. What happens to the *arahant* after death is what is experienced by the *arahant* in life. Experiencing the fourth stage of *nibbāna* they understand that this is the ultimate stage, which also happens after death. It cannot be explained in words because it is beyond mind and matter. Something beyond the sensory field cannot be expressed by the sense organs. A fourth dimensional experience cannot be represented within three dimensions. The proof is in eating the cake.

Q. Can an enlightened married person still have children?

A. Passion naturally becomes weaker as you proceed and yet you feel so contented and happy. Why worry about it? Come to that stage and the question will get answered.

Q. Is there a preferred order to list the ten *pāramīs*?

A. It is more important to develop them: the order doesn't matter.

Q. Since Vipassana is widespread, are *sotāpannas, ānāgāmīs* and *arahants* to be found today?

A. The number of meditators today is just a drop in an ocean of billions of people, and most are at the kindergarten stage: there are cases of meditators who have experienced *nibbāna,* but very few.

Q. Without offence, are you, Goenka, fully enlightened?

A. I am not an *arahant,* but without doubt on the path to becoming one. Having taken a few more steps on the path than all of you, I am competent to teach you. Walk on the path and reach the goal: that is more important than examining your teacher!

Q. Who was Ledi Sayadaw's teacher? You frequently mention the tradition where *vedanā* is fundamental: what is the name of this tradition?

A. There is no recorded history, but Ledi Sayadaw says that he learnt this technique from a monk in Mandalay. The tradition existed even before Ledi Sayadaw. Out of his many students, some started teaching and also gave importance to *vedanā.* Saya Thet taught Sayagyi U Ba Khin, among other teachers, and Sayagyi U Ba Khin had a number of students who started teaching. One is here and he gives importance to *vedanā.* This tradition gives importance to *vedanā.*

Q. About chanting...

A. Chanting is part of the duty of a Teacher, to give good vibrations, to protect the work of the students from any bad vibrations from outside. The students' job is to practice and observe, which is why they are not asked to chant. At a certain stage some are taught: between each word you are aware of sensations with *anicca,* with *sampajañña* very clearly in every pause. This, not mere chanting, gives the Dhamma vibration. It becomes part of the constant meditation of *sampajañña.* Otherwise mere chanting, which looks so easy, is just a rite, ritual or religious ceremony.

Q. If not the ego, which part of the being can give or receive *mettā?*

A. Vipassana takes you to the ultimate truth, but the Buddha wanted you to be aware of both this and the apparent truth. Both this wall and my head are ultimately vibrations but apparently solid. The wall will still break my head on impact! Ultimately there is no being, but you still give up unwholesome actions—such as hatred, aversion, ill will, and animosity—because they harm you. Generating *mettā,* love, compassion and goodwill, makes your mind better, and helps you to reach the final goal.

Q. It appears that your interpretation of the text is not as literal as it could be. How do you know that your interpretation is correct and what the Buddha intended?

A. The language is twenty-five centuries old, and meanings change. Even if they do not, what the Buddha said with his experience cannot be understood without that experience. Many translators have never practiced. We are not here to quarrel with or condemn other interpretations of the Buddha's words. As you practice, you will understand what the Buddha meant; and for now you must accept whatever you do experience.

Commentaries were written on the Buddha's words, some over 1,000 years after his death, although our research reveals that Vipassana in its pure form was lost 500 years after his death. Others were written within 500 years, but were lost except in Sri Lanka: they were again translated into Pāli, but with the translator's own interpretation. They give a clear picture of Indian society in the Buddha's time: the whole spectrum of its social, political, educational, cultural, religious and philosophical background. They often unravel obscure words by giving many synonyms. Yet while they are very helpful, if their words differ from our experience, and if in the Buddha's words we find a clear, direct explanation, then without condemning the commentaries, we have to accept the Buddha's explanation of our experience.

For instance, one tradition takes *vedanā* as only mental. It is true that *vedanā* is a mental aggregate and that *vedanānupassanā* has to be mental. But in several places the Buddha talks of *sukha* and *dukkha vedanā* on the body, as in the *Satipaṭṭhāna Sutta,* whereas *somanassa* and *domanassa vedanā* are used for the mind.

Some translations in English of the word *sampajañña,* such as "clear comprehension," have created much confusion. This suggests *sati* without *sampajañña,* the understanding with perfect *paññā.* In the Buddha's words, *viditā vedanā uppajjati,* you feel sensation coming up. Mere awareness is all right just as a start: for instance, an itch is just felt and labeled, with no understanding of *anicca*—but this is not *sampajañña.*

Similarly *sati parimukhaṃ* has been translated "keeping the attention in front." People start imagining their attention to be in front, outside the body, and the technique of *kāye kāyānupassī, vedanāsu vedanānupassī—in* the body, *in* the sensations—is lost. When our experience differs from the beliefs of other traditions, we take shelter in the Buddha's words.

The Vipassana Research Institute has been established to go through all the Buddha's words using computers; the volume of the literature is huge. Instead of remembering instances of, say, *vedanā* or *sampajāno* in 40 - 50 volumes of 300 - 400 pages each, computers are used to find the usages for examination. If differences result, we can't help it, but nor do we insist that *idaṃ saccaṃ,* "this only is the truth." There is no attachment. I understand from my direct experience of the words of the Buddha, and from this line of teachers, including those who reached very high stages. Their experience was the same. Similarly thousands of meditators around the world have had the same experience. I am therefore confident that this teaching is correct and the Buddha's way. If in doubt, practice: only practice will remove the doubts. If this technique does not suit you intellectually, then work with something else, but don't keep mixing, running here and there. If you find results with this technique, go deeper and all your questions will be answered. Even having learnt just a little Pāli, the words of the Buddha will become clear in time. You feel he is directing you. Rather than unnecessary intellectual activity, or arguments and debates, experience will clarify.

✧

You have come to a *Satipatthāna* course to experience, and not just to hear the Buddha's words or a particular teacher's interpretation. Having taken three or more courses before joining, now keep going deeper so that the Buddha's words become clear by experience. Free yourselves from all these *saṅkhāras* and start experiencing real liberation. May all of you reach the final goal of full *nibbāna.*

You are taking right steps on the right path: although long, it doesn't matter. Taking the first, the second, and in this way step by step you are bound to reach the final goal. May all of you enjoy the real happiness and peace of liberation.

May all beings be happy.

List of Abbreviations

abl.	ablative
adv.	adverb
caus.	causative
dat.	dative
i.e.	id est (that is)
fig.	figurative(ly)
fpp.	future passive participle
fr.	from
gen.	genitive
ger.	gerund
lit.	literally
loc.	locative
neg.	negative
opp.	opposite
opt.	optative
pass.	passive
pp.	past participle
pres. p.	present participle
vb.	verb

Glossary

A

abhijjhā	craving, covetousness
abhinandati	rejoice, find pleasure or delight in, approve of, be pleased with
ābhujitvā	having bent in, folded (the legs)
abyāpāda	without hatred, without aversion
adhiṭṭhāna	strong determination
adhigama	attainment, acquisition
adho	below
ādīnava	danger, disadvantage
adukkhamasukha	neither pleasant nor unpleasant, neutral
ajjhatta	inside
ajjhattika	arises from within, interior, inwardly
akusala	improper, wrong, unwholesome
anāgāmī	nonreturner (third stage of an *ariya*)
anālaya	detachment [opp. *ālaya*: settling place, clinging]
anāsava	one who is free from *āsavas,* i.e.: an arahant
anatīta	unavoidable, inescapable
anissita	unsupported, detached, free [opp. of *nissita:* hanging on, dependent on]
aññā	knowledge, insight, recognition, perfect knowledge
anumāna	inference
anuppādo	non-arising
anuppanna	not arisen [opp. of *uppanna*]
āpo	water
ārabhati	begin, start, undertake, attempt
arahant	fully liberated person
ariya	noble

asāta	disagreeable
asammosa	absence of confusion
āsava	intoxicating secretion, intoxication of the mind
asesa	without remnant, entirely, completely
assasati	breathes in
assutavā	not having heard, ignorant
asuci	unclean, impure
ātāpī	ardent
aṭṭhaṅgika	eightfold
attā	(one's) self
attano	yourself, oneself (gen. and dat. of *atta,* self)
atthaṅgama	annihilation, disappearance
avihiṃsa	absence of violence, without cruelty
ayaṃ	this
āyatana	sphere of sense, sense door, sense object
āyatiṃ	in future [adv.]

B

bāhira	outer, external
bahiddhā	outside
bala	strength
bhāvī	[fr. *bhava:* becoming]
bhāvanā	developing, producing, cultivation by mind, mentally dwelling on
bhāvanā-mayā	brought about by practice
bhāvetabba	should be developed
bhūta	become [pp. of *bhavati*]
bhaṅga	total dissolution
bhagavā	fortunate, illustrious, sublime (hence "Lord")
bheda	breaking up, disjunction
bhikkhave	O *bhikkhus* [voc. pl. of *bhikku*]

bhikkhu	meditator, monk
bhiyyobhāva	become more
bojjhaṅga	factor of enlightenment [lit. *bodhi-anga:* limb of enlightenment]
byādhi	disease, sickness
byāpāda	aversion, ill-will

C

ca	and
cāga	abandoning, giving up, renunciation
cakkhu	eye
cattāro	four
cetasika	belonging to *cetas,* mental, mental contents
cha	six
chanda	impulse, intention, resolution, will
cintā-mayā	consisting of intellectual understanding
cittānupassī	continuously observing the mind
cittānupassana	observation of mind
citta	mind
citte	in the mind [loc. of *citta*]

D

dhāreti	contain, hold, carry, possess
dhātu	element [abl. *dhātuso:* according to one's nature]
dhammānupassī	continuously observing mental contents
dhammānupassana	observation of mental contents
dhammesu	in the mental contents [loc. of *dhammā*]
dhañña	grain
dhunamāna	[Pres.p. *dhunati:* shake off, remove, destroy]
dīgha	long, deep

diṭṭha	seen
domanassa	unpleasant mental feeling, grief, aversion
dosa	hatred, aversion

E

ekāyana	one and only way, direct way
ettha	here, in this place, in this matter
evaṃ	thus, in this way

G

gandha	smell
gāthā	verse
ghāna	nose
gotrabhū	"become of the lineage"

H

hoti	is

I

icchā	wish, longing, desire
idha	here, now, in this connection
imasmiṃ	in this, with reference to this
indriya	faculty, function [re: sense perception], directing principle, force
iriyāpatha	posture [of the body]

J

jānāti	knows
janati	bring forth, produce [caus. of *janati:* be born]
jāti	born, become [pp. of *janati*]
jhāna	mental absorption
jivhā	tongue
jīvita	lifetime, living, livelihood

K

kalāpa	bunch, collection, group of qualities
kāma	pleasure, sense desire
kāmacchanda	sense-desire, sensual pleasure, excitement
kata	done, made
kathaṃ	how?
kattha	where? where to? whither?
kaya	body
kāyānupassī	continuously observing the body
kāyānupassanā	observation of body
kāya-saṅkhāra	activity of the body
kāyasmiṃ	in the body [loc. of *kāya*]
kāye	in the body [loc. of *kāya*]
kesa	hair of the head
kevala	alone, whole, complete
kevalaparipuṇṇa	complete and perfect
kevalaparisuddha	complete and pure
khandha	mass, bulk, collection, aggregate
kiñci	anything
kukkucca	remorse, scruple, worry
kusala	good, right, wholesome

L

labhati	get, receive, obtain, acquire
lakkhaṇa	mark, characteristic
loka	plane of existence, mind-matter phenomenon

M

magga	path, way
mahā	big, great
mahaggata	enlarged, become great, lofty
mano	mind
manasikāra	reflection on, contemplation
matta	by measure, as much as, mere, only

matthaka	head
me	by me
micchā	wrong
middha	drowsiness, torpor
moha	ignorance, delusion
mukha	mouth, face, entrance
musā	falsely, wrongly
mutti	release, freedom, emancipation

N

na	not
nāma	mind
nandi	enjoyment, delight
ñāṇa	knowledge
nānappakkāra	various, manifold
nātha	refuge, help, protector
natthi	is not [*na atthi*]
nava	nine
ñāya	truth, system, right conduct
nirāmisa	pure, without attachment [opp. *sāmisa*]
nirodha	eradication, cessation
nirujjhati	is eradicated, ceases
nisīdati	sit, be seated
nisinno	seated
nīvaraṇa	hindrance, obstacle, curtain
nivisati	enter, stop, settle down on, resort to, establish oneself

O

okkhitta	downcast

P

paccakkha	evident, clear, present
paccattaṃ	separately, individually
paccavekkhati	contemplate, look upon, consider

paccaya	cause, condition, foundation
paccupaṭṭhita	become established
padahati	strive, exert
pādatala	sole of the foot
paggaṇhāti	take up, exert, apply (the mind) vigorously
pahāna	giving up, abandoning [fr. *pajahati*, pass. *pahīyati*]
pajānati	comes to know, understands properly, understands with wisdom
pakāra	mode, manner
pallaṅka	sitting cross-legged
pana	again, further
pāṇātipāta	killing, murder, destruction of a life
pañca	five
pañcupādānakkhandhā	five aggregates of clinging
paññatti	concept, manifestation
paṇḍita	wise person
paṇihitaṃ	put forth, applied, disposed [pp. of *paṇidahati*]
pāpa	evil
pāpaka	bad
pāramī	perfection
pāripūrī	fulfillment, completion, consummation
pārisuddhi	purity
parāmāsa	attachment
paraṃ	further
parideva	crying, lamentation
parijānāti	completely understands
parimukha	around the mouth
pariññāta	understood to its end
paripāka	ripeness, decay
pariyanta	bounded by, limited by, surrounded
pariyatti	theoretical knowledge
passaddhi	calm, tranquillity

passambhaya	calming, quieting
passasati	breathes out [1st pers.: *passasāmī;* 1st pers. fut.: *passasissāmī*]
passati	sees
passeyya	should see, would see [opt., fr. *passati:* see]
paṭhavī	earth
paṭṭhāna	extensively established (with wisdom)
paṭicca	because of, dependent on
paṭikūla	loathsome
paṭinissagga	giving up, forsaking, rejection, renunciation
paṭipadā	path, way, means of reaching a destination
paṭipatti	practice
paṭisaṃvedī	experiences, feels
paṭissati	awareness
paṭivedha	piercing, penetrating knowledge, insight
pattabba	to be gained, attained, won
phala	fruit
phassa	contact
phoṭṭhabba	touch
pisuṇa	back-biting, malicious, calumnious
pīti	rapture, bliss
piya	dear, beloved, pleasant, agreeable [opp. *appiya*]
ponobbhavikā	leading to rebirth
puna	again
pūra	full of

R

rāga	craving, passion
rajo	dust, dirt, impurity
rasa	taste

rassa	short, shallow
riñcati	abandon, neglect, miss
rūpa	matter

S

sabba	all, every
sabhāva	nature, disposition, truth
sacca	truth, real
sacchikātabba	to be seen, realized
sacchikata	seen, realized, experienced for oneself [pp. of *sacchikaroti*]
sacchikiriyā	experiencing, realizing, making true
sadda	sound, word
saddhā	faith, devotion, confidence
saddhiṃ	together
sadosa	with aversion [opp. *vītadosa*]
sakadāgāmī	once-returner (second stage of an ariya)
saḷāyatana	six sense-spheres, both internal (the sense faculty) and external (the object sensed)
samādhija	resulting from concentration
samāhita	collected, composed, attentive
samatikkama	passing beyond, overcoming, transcending
samaya	time
samudaya	arising
sāmisa	impure, of the flesh, with attachment [opp. *nirāmisa*]
saṅkhitta	collected, attentive [opp. *vikkhitta:* scattered]
sammā	right, proper, perfect
samoha	with delusion [opp. *vītamoha*]
sampajāna	with *sampajañña*
sampajañña	constant thorough understanding of impermanence

sampajānakārī	practicing *sampajañña* (*kāri*: doing)
sampasādana	serenity
sampayoga	union, association
samphappalāpa	frivolous talk
samphassa	contact
samphassaja	resulting from contact
samudaya	arising
samudayasacca	truth of arising
saṃyojana	bond, fetter
sañcetanā	thought, cogitation, intention, reaction
saṅkhāra	mental aggregate of reaction, mental formation, volitional activity, mental conditioning
saṅkhittena	in short, concisely
saññā	perception, recognition
santa	is [pres.part. of *atthi*] [opp. *asanta:* is not]
sarāga	with craving [opp. *vītarāga*]
sāta	pleasant, agreeable [opp. *asāta*]
sati	awareness
satimā	with awareness
satipaṭṭhāna	establishing of awareness
sato	aware
satta	individual, living sentient being
satta	seven
sauttara	surpassable, inferior [opp. *anuttara:* "nothing higher"]
sāvaka	hearer, disciple
sikkhati	learns, trains oneself
soka	burning grief, sorrow
somanassa	pleasant mental feeling, happiness
sotāpanna	stream-enterer (first stage of an *ariya*)
sota	stream
sota	ear

sukha	pleasant, happy
supaṭipanna	having practiced well
suta	heard
sutavā	having heard
sutta	discourse [lit. thread]

T

taca	skin
taṇhā	craving, thirst, hunger, excitement, fever
tato	from this, in this
tatratatrābhinandinī	finding delight here, there and all around
tejo	fire
tesaṃ	their
ṭhāna	established, set up, condition, state
ṭhita	upright, firm, standing [pp. of *tiṭṭhati:* stand]
thina	stiffness, mental deficiency, inertia
ṭhiti	stability, continuance, immobility, persistence
ti	[a particle denoting the end of a quotation]
tipiṭaka	three divisions of the teachings

U

ubhaya	both, twofold
uddhaṃ	above
uddhacca	agitation, over-balancing, excitement, distraction, flurry
uju	straight, erect
upādāna	grasping, clinging, support, attachment,
upādānakkhandha	aggregate of clinging
upādi	materially determined [see *upādāna*], substratum of being

upādiyati — take hold of, grasp, cling to
upaṭṭhapetvā — having established, caused to be present [ger. causative of *upaṭṭhahati:* stands near]
upasaṃharati — concentrate, collect, consider
upasampajja — having attained, entered on, acquired [ger. of *upasampajjati*]
upāyāsa — trouble, tribulation, disturbance, distress
upekkhā — equanimity
upekkhako — equanimous, with equanimity
uppāda — coming into existence, appearance, birth, arising
uppajjamāna — arising [pres.p. of *uppajjati*]
uppajjati — arise, be produced, be born, come into existence
uppajjitvā — arisen
uppanna — born, reborn, arisen, produced [pp. of uppajjati]
uppanna — arisen [pp. of uppajjati]

V

vā — or
vāca — speech
vata — vow, religious observance
vaya — passing away
vāyāma — striving, effort, exertion, endeavor
vāyamati — make effort
vāyo — air, wind
vedagu — one with highest knowledge
vedanānupassī — continuously observing sensations
vedanānupassanā — observation of sensations
vedanāsu — in the sensations [loc. of *vedanā*]
vedayati — feel, experience a sensation or feeling (usually with *vedanā*)

veditabba	to be experienced, understood, known [fpp. of *vedeti*]
vepulla	full development, abundance, plenty, fullness
veramaṇī	abstaining from
vibhava	non-existence, cessation of life, annihilation
vicāra	sustained mental application, rolling in thoughts
vicaya	investigation
vicikicchā	doubt, perplexity, uncertainty
vihārin	dwelling, living, being in a certain condition
viharati	lives, dwells [lit. takes out (the impurities)]
vikkhittaka	scattered, dismembered
vimutta	freed, liberated [opp. *a-vimutta:* not freed]
vinīlaka	bluish-black, discolored
vinaya	discipline, code of conduct [for monks]
vineyya	keeping away, detached [fr. *vineti:* remove, give up, instruct, train]
viññāṇa	consciousness
vippayoga	separation
virāga	absence of desire [*rāga*], disgust, destruction of passions, waning, purifying, emancipation
viriya	effort
visesa	mark, distinction, characteristic
visuddhi	purity, brightness
vitakka	initial mental application, thought conception
viveka	separation, seclusion, discrimination
vivicca	having become separated or isolated from

vuccati	is called
vūpasama	calming

Y

yathā	as, how
yathābhūtaṃ	as it is
yāvadeva	as far as, as long as

Pāli Passages Quoted In the Discourses

Paññatti ṭhapetvā visesena passati'ti vipassanā.

—Ledi Sayadaw,
Paramattha Dīpanī

Vedanā-samosaraṇā sabbe dhammā.

—Mūlaka-sutta,
Aṅguttara-nikāya, III,158

Diṭṭe diṭṭhamattaṃ bhavissati,
sute sutamattaṃ bhavissati,
mute mutamattaṃ bhavissati,
viññate viññātamattaṃ bhavissati.

—Mālukyaputta-sutta, Saṃyutta-nikāya,
Salāyatana-vagga 2, 77

Seyyathāpi, bhikkhave, ākāse vividhā vātā vāyanti. purathima pi vātā vāyanti, pacchimā pi vātā vāyanti, uttarā pi vātā vāyanti, dakkhiṇa pi vātā vāyanti, sarajā pi vātā vāyanti, arajā pi vātā vāyanti, sītā pi vātā vāyanti, uṇhā pi vātā vāyanti, parittā pi vātā vāyanti, adhimattā pi vātā vāyanti. Evameva kho, bhikkhave, imasmiṃ kāyasmiṃ vividhā vedanā uppajjanti, sukhā pi vedanā uppajjanti, dukkhā pi vedanā uppajjanti, adukkhamasukhā pi vedanā uppajjantī ti....

Yato ca bhikkhu ātāpī sampajaññaṃ na riñcati,
tato so vedanā sabbā parijānāti paṇḍito;

So vedanā pariññāya diṭṭhe dhamme anāsavo,
kāyassa bhedā Dhammaṭṭho, saṅkhyaṃ nopeti vedagū.

—Paṭhama-ākāsa-sutta, Saṃyutta-nikāya,
Salāyatana-vagga 2, 212

English Translation of Pāli Passages

Having removed apparent reality, observing reality in its true characteristic, this is *vipassanā.*

Everything that arises in the mind is accompanied by sensation.

In the seen there will be merely the seen;
in the heard, merely the heard;
in the smelled, the tasted and touched, merely the smelled, tasted, touched;
in the cognized, there will be merely the cognized.

Through the sky blow many different winds, from east and west, from north and south, dust-laden or dustless, cold or hot, fierce gales or gentle breezes many winds blow. In the same way, in the body sensations arise, pleasant, unpleasant, or neutral....

When a meditator practicing ardently, does not, miss his faculty of thorough understanding,
such a wise one fully understands all sensations.
And having completely understood them, he becomes freed from all impurities.
On the breaking up of the body, such a person, being established in Dhamma and understanding sensations perfectly, attains the indescribable stage beyond the conditioned world.

Sabba kamma jahassa bhikkhuno,
dhunamānassa pure kataṃ rajaṃ;
amamassa ṭhitassa tādino,
attho natthi janaṃ lapetave.

—Khuddaka-nikaya,Udāna 3.1, 91-92

Aniccā vata saṅkhāra,
uppādavaya-dhammino;
uppajjitvā nirujjhanti,
tesaṃ vūpasamo sukho.

—Mahāparinibbāna-sutta,
Digha-nikaya 2.3, 221

Paṭicca-samuppāda

Anuloma:

Avijjā-paccayā saṅkhārā;
saṅkhāra-paccayā viññāṇaṃ;
viññāṇa-paccayā nāma-rūpaṃ;
nāma-rūpa-paccayā saḷāyatanaṃ;
saḷāyatana-paccayā phasso;
phassa-paccayā vedanā;
vedanā-paccayā taṇhā;
taṇhā-paccayā upādānaṃ;
upādāna-paccayā bhavo;
bhava-paccayā jāti;
jāti-paccayā jarā-maraṇaṃ-soka-parideva-dukkha-
domanassupāyāsā sambhavanti.

Evame-tassa kevalassa dukkhakkhandhassa
samudayo hoti.

—Paṭicca-samuppāda-sutta,
Saṃyutta-nikāya, XII (I), 1

The monk who does not make new *kamma*,
and combs out old defilements as they arise;
has reached that meditative state where there remains no 'I' or 'mine'.
For him mere babbling makes no sense.
Engrossed in silent practice he is bent.

Impermanent truly are compounded things,
by nature arising and passing away
having arisen, when they are extinguished,
their eradication brings happiness.

Chain of Conditioned Arising

Forward Order:

With the base of ignorance, reaction arises;
with the base of reaction, consciousness arises;
with the base of consciousness, mind and body arise;
with the base of mind and body, the six senses arise;
with the base of the six senses, contact arises;
with the base of contact, sensation arises;
with the base of sensation, craving and aversion arise;
with the base of craving and aversion, attachment arises;
with the base of attachment, the process of becoming arises;
with the base of the process of becoming, birth arises;
with the base of birth, aging and death arise, together with sorrow, lamentation, physical and mental sufferings and tribulations.

Thus arises this entire mass of suffering.

Vipassana Meditation Centers

Courses of Vipassana meditation in the tradition of Sayagyi U Ba Khin as taught by S. N. Goenka are held regularly in many countries around the world.

Information, worldwide schedules and application forms are available from the Vipassana website:

www.dhamma.org

ABOUT PARIYATTI

Pariyatti is dedicated to providing affordable access to authentic teachings of the Buddha about the Dhamma theory (*pariyatti*) and practice (*paṭipatti*) of Vipassana meditation. A 501(c)(3) non-profit charitable organization since 2002, Pariyatti is sustained by contributions from individuals who appreciate and want to share the incalculable value of the Dhamma teachings. We invite you to visit www.pariyatti.org to learn about our programs, services, and ways to support publishing and other undertakings.

Pariyatti Publishing Imprints

Vipassana *Research Publications* (focus on Vipassana as taught by S.N. Goenka in the tradition of Sayagyi U Ba Khin)

BPS Pariyatti Editions (selected titles from the Buddhist Publication Society, copublished by Pariyatti in the Americas)

Pariyatti Digital Editions (audio and video titles, including discourses)

Pariyatti Press (classic titles returned to print and inspirational writing by contemporary authors)

Pariyatti enriches the world by

- disseminating the words of the Buddha,
- providing sustenance for the seeker's journey,
- illuminating the meditator's path.